How to Chair a Department

How to Chair a Department

Kevin Dettmar

Johns Hopkins University Press • *Baltimore*

Johns Hopkins University Press
2715 North Charles Street
Baltimore, Maryland 21218-4363
www.press.jhu.edu

Library of Congress Cataloging-in-Publication Data

Names: Dettmar, Kevin J. H., 1958- author.
Title: How to chair a department / Kevin Dettmar.
Description: Baltimore : Johns Hopkins University Press, 2022. | Series: Higher ed
    leadership essentials | Includes bibliographical references and index.
Identifiers: LCCN 2022005040 (print) | LCCN 2022005041 (ebook) |
    ISBN 9781421445236 (paperback) | ISBN 9781421445243 (ebook)
Subjects: LCSH: College department heads—United States—Handbooks,
    manuals, etc. | Universities and colleges—United States—Departments—
    Handbooks, manuals, etc.
Classification: LCC LB2341 .D417 2022 (print) | LCC LB2341 (ebook) |
    DDC 378.1/010973—dc23/eng/20220316
LC record available at https://lccn.loc.gov/2022005040
LC ebook record available at https://lccn.loc.gov/2022005041

A catalog record for this book is available from the British Library.

*Special discounts are available for bulk purchases of this book. For more information,
please contact Special Sales at specialsales@jh.edu.*

Contents

Acknowledgments

My heartfelt thanks go out especially to three groups of colleagues who together have taught me almost everything I know about chairing a department:

- Wise faculty colleagues I served alongside: Martin Jacobi, Beth Daniell, Lee Morrissey, Jane Cogie, and Ed Brunner
- Wise department chairs I served under: Frank Day and Oona Eisenstadt
- Wise deans it was a pleasure to serve with: Shirley Clay Scott, Gary Kates, Cecilia Conrad, Betsy Crighton, Janice Hudgings, and Bob Gaines

For more systematic and focused coaching, I am above all grateful to David Laurence and the late Doug Steward of the Association of Departments of English. The ADE Summer Seminars provided invaluable support in my early days of chairing a department. Their invitations to lead sessions on faculty hiring, dealing with conflict, and maintaining a research profile, and opportunities to lead the daylong new chairs' workshops, helped me think through much of the material that appears in these pages. I learned more from my fellow English department chairs at those annual meetings than I can hope to acknowledge here.

I'm happy to express my gratitude to the two anonymous press readers who took this manuscript and made it much better. Beyond that, I'm deeply indebted to my colleague, friend, and back-fence neighbor Dan O'Leary, professor of chemistry at Pomona College, who read the full manuscript and told me when I was being parochial.

I'm grateful to my colleague George Justice at Arizona State, author of *How to Be a Dean* in this series, who put my name forward for this project, and to Greg Britton at Johns Hopkins University Press, who put the bug in my ear and then did it again.

Warm thanks to my longtime editor at the *Chronicle of Higher Education* (now emerita) Jean Tamarin, who provided a space for me to teach myself many of these lessons in writing and who taught me how to do so in language that might connect with others.

Part of chapter 1 is adapted from "What We Waste When Faculty Hiring Goes Wrong," *Chronicle of Higher Education*, December 17, 2004. Thanks to the publisher for permission to reuse here. Chapter 10 originally appeared in *ADE Bulletin* 154 (2015): 72-76. Thanks to the editors for permission to reuse here. A version of the epilogue was presented as "Scholarly Community and the Gift Economy" in the "State of the Profession" colloquium series at the University of Colorado, Boulder, in November 2007, at the invitation of Jeffrey Robinson.

Odds and sods from my essay "Don't Cry for Me, Academia" (*Chronicle of Higher Education*, June 27, 2016) appear at regular if unpredictable intervals throughout. Thanks to the publishers for permitting me to plagiarize myself.

Thanks to Caren Irr for allowing me to reprint her thoughts on herding cats.

This book is dedicated to my first and best chair, Frank Day.

How to Chair a Department

Introduction

"Congratulations—or should I say *condolences*?" It's a sentiment every newly selected department chair has heard. (And heard and heard and heard, and you're supposed to chuckle gamely and pretend that it's witty *every time*.) If you're reading this book, odds are it's because you've been tapped yourself (and if you're lucky, perhaps one of the wags wishing you good luck with "herding the cats" went a step further and bought the book for you). Or you're newly tenured in a department with a shallow leadership bench and can, to mix metaphors, read the tea leaves: having been forewarned, you're trying to get forearmed. Or *nel mezzo del cammin di tua vita*,* the challenges, responsibilities, and rewards of the chair's role are exerting their siren call. Or maybe after having attempted to chair for a bit, you're starting to realize that nothing in your professional training has prepared you for this.

---

*"Midway through the journey of your life," a paraphrase of the opening of Dante's *Divine Comedy*. Nerd alert: literature professor at work.

And it's true: nothing in graduate training readies us for the important leadership role of chairing an academic department. By all appearances, the profession runs on an economy of prestige; we are taught (both explicitly and implicitly) that to succeed is to become a charismatic and beloved teacher and/or world-renowned scholar or artist.* No one pursues a graduate degree in order to become a department chair. And yet many—most?—of us will serve in that capacity at some point in our careers. If we posit (for argument's sake) an average-size department of 20 faculty members, a typical career of 35 years, and a chair's term of 3 years, there's nearly a 60% chance of any given faculty member serving a term. Done well, it's work that can make a profound difference in the professional lives of your colleagues and the educational experience of your students; done poorly, it can have equally powerful effects. But few who do the work will ever receive significant professional training to develop the requisite skills.†

To make matters worse, we often choose our department chairs on rather faulty grounds. A college or university president is normally chosen based on their‡ demonstrated ability as a provost or dean, or at least as an effective fundraiser. Most provosts boast accomplished records as academic deans, and most academic deans will have proven their mettle in the roles of associate dean or successful chair of a large department. But for many new

*Because the locution becomes tedious, although I will often refer to "research and creative activity," any time I use the terms "research" or "scholarship," I mean to include the work of artists, creators, and makers.

†In my own discipline of English, we are fortunate to have the Association of Departments of English Summer Seminars, which provide wide-ranging and practical support for both new and veteran department chairs. I'm not aware that similar supports exist for chairs in other disciplines, and the one interdisciplinary chairs workshop I attended was conducted at such a general level as to be practically useless to me.

‡Unless referring to an individual whose gender I'm making plain, I use the pronouns they/them/their and themself (singular reflexive) or themselves (plural reflexive).

chairs, the appointment marks their first formal academic leadership assignment. Indeed, I suspect that faculty colleagues are often appointed to chair their departments based on their reputations as charismatic teachers or innovative researchers or artists. None of these achievements is a good proxy for the gifts, skills, and disposition that make a person a good department chair.*

Much of what an effective department chair does can be taught and learned. However, the differences between departments can be vast; think of the distinct challenges involved in chairing the molecular biology department at a large research university, the music department in a school for the performing arts or conservatory, the foreign languages department at a community college, and the economics department at a small liberal arts college. In each case, the roles and the challenges are fundamentally of the same nature, even though the scale and local conditions vary. Most experienced faculty members with a modicum of common sense and interpersonal skill can chair their department successfully for the typical three-year term by keeping in mind the advice found in the chapters that follow.

To do a really transformative job—to be not just an adequate but an outstanding chair—two more things are required, two personal commitments. I think of them as optional; not all of those who end up doing the work of chairing do so willingly, and for some the role is something to be endured rather than mastered. That's fine: no judgment here. But to really excel at this thing—not just to enhance the work of your colleagues and the experience of your students (although those are huge) but additionally to reap from the role the personal reward that's possible—you'll have to adjust your thinking in two significant ways.

---

*My own experience of having twice been hired from the outside as a department chair suggests that even in a national search for a chair, where the institution is committing considerable resources (including, typically, a tenure line), the process is guided to a much greater degree by a scholarly and teaching agenda than by an administrative one.

First, you'll have to recognize that the role of the department chair requires acting as what I call the designated grown-up.* You're the bad cop, the buzzkill, the wet blanket, the reality principle. The chair's role exists, in part, to insulate the rest of the faculty from having to deal with the exigencies of institutional budgets, personnel paperwork, accreditation, strategic planning, and so on; the chair is responsible for the department's annual report to the dean *so their faculty colleagues don't have to be*. Which means, necessarily, that you're giving up no small part of the freedom that made joining the professoriate so attractive to begin with. Great chairs, I believe, accept the role of designated grown-up for a time to protect the freedom of their faculty colleagues to have big, impractical—sometimes brilliant—dreams. Because faculty members know that their department chair will deliver a budget to the dean that balances income and expenses and keeps the photocopier or autoclave running, they're free to think outside the box, and sometimes, they arrive at truly visionary ideas that purely pragmatic thinking would never have given birth to. So as chair, you're often playing the role of naysayer, but sometimes you have the privilege of being the yeasayer.

I remember a faculty meeting some years ago in which a brilliant colleague who is very creative in the ways they think about supporting junior faculty spitballed an idea: what if we offered to solicit two confidential outside evaluations of our tenure-track colleagues' first-book manuscripts and then brought those two experts to campus for consultation with the author before they submitted their book to a publisher? (This was in a department that effectively requires a book for tenure.) These reviews would be conveyed to the young faculty member alone, for their eyes only. Wouldn't that put our junior colleagues in a much stronger position to secure contracts for their books as they were preparing for tenure review? To be honest, this struck me, at first blush, as an exciting idea—and completely impossible.

*I'll have more to say about this in chapter 8.

This was proposed at an institution that doesn't even pay an honorarium to outside reviewers of tenure and promotion dossiers, whereas this professional development package, which would require honoraria, travel, lodging, and meals for two, would likely come to $3,000. Three thousand dollars is a lot of money, but it's a bargain when measured against the costs of losing a promising young scholar—the loss of seven years' institutional investment in their professional development (which at the institution in question includes a full-year professional-development leave for junior faculty) and the expense of running a new search and mentoring a new faculty member. If I had started out with my nose in the budget, I would never have been able to imagine a program like this. Instead, after taking the pressure off my colleagues to be reasonable (because we all knew that was my job), we put together something really terrific. To paraphrase Oscar Wilde: faculty are all under the budget, but some of us are looking at the stars.

If you're currently a department chair, someone earlier in your career did (or should have done) this work for you. When your term as chair is up, someone else will come take the yoke and relieve you of the responsibility. It's the circle of administrative life. But for now, the job's yours—embrace it. Know too that to the extent that you successfully siphon off the administrative responsibilities* that faculty seem almost instinctively to avoid, you'll inevitably create some distance between your colleagues and yourself. It will happen whether you will it or not. If you at least understand it for what it is, you will recognize that it's nothing personal. For department chairs it's right there in the title: while *president*, *provost*, and *dean* denominate roles and the people that hold them, a *chair* is first and foremost a thing, an everyday household object.

Second, the most effective department chairs see their work as a profound form of service, a gift they can give to their colleagues.

*The term "administrivia" might not be quite fair, but let's just acknowledge that it's out there, and it *is* kind of catchy.

(I'll return to this in the epilogue.) Yes, it is possible to chair a department without much real personal sacrifice, but I'm not sure it's possible to do it really well that way. Scholars, we may as well admit, are rather selfish when it comes to their work: we're taught early on to protect our time. (Making things even worse, unlike many of our colleagues in the sciences and social sciences, those of us in the humanities tend to pursue projects that are best tackled alone.)* Chairing really well asks that we put that impulse to protect our time on hold, at least for a spell, asks that we genuinely put the well-being of our colleagues (which is to say, in many cases, their professional development) above our own and learn to celebrate their triumphs in lieu of our own, to live our professional lives (for a time, to a degree) vicariously through their successes.†

Chairing your department doesn't require these sacrifices, these significant changes in your attitude toward and understanding of your work, but real leadership, I'm persuaded, does. Some of us move into the chair's role precisely because we feel a stirring to be of service to our colleagues or perhaps to pay back (and pay forward) gifts of service that made possible the careers we now enjoy. Some of us, having accepted the assignment only out of a sense of obligation, come to discover in it something like a calling.

Chairing is not for everyone, although many of us will need to do it anyway. If that's your situation, I hope that you may none-

*I'm still haunted by a tableau from one of the universities where I was a student. A faculty mentor whose weekly office hour (singular) was 4–5 p.m. on Friday held it in their basement office with the lights off and the door closed. A small transom window provided the office's only illumination. To consult with them, one had to knock on that intimidating door and wait for them to peer through the narrow crack they opened to identify you and grudgingly "invite" you in. They were an incredibly prolific scholar.

†This is not to suggest, however, that a term as chair should be understood as a necessary hiatus from all professional activity. Indeed, I would argue that to treat it this way does a grave disservice to yourself and your colleagues. In chapter 10, I'll explore strategies for maintaining a scholarly or artistic profile while chairing.

theless discover in it some of the great reward that comes from serving colleagues and discover some useful advice in these pages for doing the job well. For if prestige is the official currency the academy runs on, service—the kind exemplified by the work of the department chair—is its subterranean gift economy, an underground stream that quietly nourishes the entire enterprise.

A word on approach: I've spent more than half of my professional career in various academic leadership roles, but I'm not a student of the higher education leadership literature. With the exception of chapter 10, which was written in collaboration with a colleague who is more conversant with the research in the field, this book grows out of experience rather than study and you'll find very few references to other work in the field. What I know about chairing a department I know from having chaired three very different departments at two very different kinds of institutions for a total of fourteen years and what I learned at the Harvard Institutes for Higher Education's Management Development Program, many summer seminars hosted by the Association of Departments of English, and countless pieces over the years in the *Chronicle of Higher Education* and *Inside Higher Ed*. It's that experience that I hope to communicate here.

One consequence is that you'll frequently encounter the first-person pronoun, as in the previous sentence. Often when I encounter this in academic writing, I read it as a sign of ego (and of course, literally, it is that). But I hope that in this book it can function modestly: instead of pretending that things that I think I know based only on my own experience are universal truths, I'll try to remind readers that the advice offered here grows out of experiences that are by their nature personal (though I hope not wholly idiosyncratic). I've worked at research universities, a private religious institution, and a liberal arts college, but all my experience comes from four-year institutions. My relative unfamiliarity with the two-year system is a shortcoming I can only acknowledge. Likewise, I've been fortunate to work only in institutions that still, despite all the pressures to the contrary, hire faculty into tenure-track positions. I've worked with and been the chair of non-tenure-track faculty. However, except for a first year as a visiting assistant professor, I've never been off the tenure track. I have tried to be mindful of those who work without the job security and career supports of the tenure track and beg your forgiveness in advance for any places remaining where I've been blind to the professional privilege I've enjoyed. Finally, although each of my previous faculty appointments involved teaching graduate students, I have touched only glancingly here on a chair's additional responsibilities in departments that grant graduate degrees. Those differences are significant enough to warrant treatment on their own, perhaps in a book on directing a graduate program.

This book also reads a bit like a nonfiction *roman à clef*—a *manuel à clef*, I suppose. Every observation, every piece of advice, has a story, an experience, and above all a face behind it: chairs I was privileged to work under, faculty I was trusted to lead. That said, as they warn you at the movies, names, characters, departments, institutions and incidents portrayed here are products of the author's imagination. Any resemblance to actual persons living or dead or to actual events or institutions is purely coincidental.

The chapters that follow—eleven gerunds, followed at the book's close by something very like a homily—tackle the fundamental areas of responsibility of the chair's role.

Chapter 1

Hiring Faculty

Hiring new and replacement faculty is some of the most important work an academic department does, and as chair, providing leadership and guidance through that complex process is some of the most important work you'll do. Although such positions are becoming increasingly rare, a faculty appointment to the tenure track represents your institution's potential commitment over three decades or more and amounting to several million dollars to the career of an academic. In turn, your new colleague will be expected to be a dedicated and inspirational teacher, perhaps (depending on institutional type) an innovative scholar or creator, and a contributor through their service work to the larger mission of the department, the college or university, and the profession. Today, the majority of new appointments are for non-tenure-track faculty, and while the contract terms and working conditions for these positions are normally less advantageous, these too represent an opportunity for a department to build for its future and to bring on colleagues who ideally will be with them for years and years to come. Apart from campus buildings, faculty are the longest-term and most expensive investments a college or university makes (and sometimes they last longer than the buildings).

Faculty hiring is important work, then, but it's a challenge to do it well. This is captured anecdotally in two contradictory laments you'll hear from chairs during what we used to call hiring season. (Across the disciplines, the decoupling of interviews from the field's annual convention has upended the traditional hiring calendar.) One group of lucky chairs will complain about how time consuming and difficult (and, often, acrimonious) their current faculty search is proving to be and the others will complain that they haven't been granted permission by the administration to undertake that time-consuming, difficult, acrimonious work. Although the process will be overseen to some degree by the dean's or provost's office and the human resources unit, the chair is the department member ultimately responsible for seeing that the process runs with integrity and produces a good result. Your college or university employs staff who specialize in diversity, equity, and inclusion (DEI) work and who will consult with you throughout the hiring process to ensure that the search rewards diversity, promotes equity, and fosters inclusion. But those considerations operate at a superdisciplinary level; your campus's DEI officer does not have the knowledge of your discipline necessary to ensure that your search committee fairly recognizes and rewards disciplinary knowledge and achievement. The chair will not normally oversee every part of the search process. Most often, faculty colleagues with more relevant expertise and experience will be in a better position to vet the candidates' qualifications as scholars and teachers, for instance. But in the end, the chair must ensure that the process is fair and produces the candidate best suited to meet the current and future needs of the department.

Identifying the Need

Most commonly, three possible things (which frequently overlap) alert a department to the need for a faculty search: the loss of a colleague, the department's inability to staff courses in the curriculum adequately, and/or a perceived lack of coverage in all necessary areas of the discipline. Quite often the departure of a key colleague can create both staffing and field-coverage problems.

Not all faculty members understand their role (and the role of their specializations) in the department in the same way. I remember two senior faculty members in my first tenure-track appointment who seemed to me, in their divergent attitudes, to sum up the range of approaches to thinking about faculty colleagues. One was a Renaissance scholar with a specialty in Shakespeare. Whenever there was the even remotest chance of hiring in the department, they argued for hiring another Shakespearean (and the department already had three). They were an unembarrassed apologist for the centrality of their specialization within the discipline, and the prospect of more colleagues within their specialty, a deeper cast of players, gladdened their heart. The other was a scholar of English Romantic poetry. Even in a rather large department (more than 40 full-time faculty), they insisted that no other Romanticist would be hired while they were there. (In retrospect, there's something suspiciously Romantic about this insistence on isolation.) They wanted the field to themself, a field over which they might wander "lonely as a cloud"; they *were* a field unto themself, chanting their ode to solitude.

The scholarly contours of a department shift over time, changing with the interests of its current members, new directions in the field, strategic initiatives of the college or university, and the interests and passions of undergraduate and graduate students. For a department to remain vital, new hiring must respond to those shifts. Often, however, departments almost reflexively decide to replace a departing colleague with another of the same stripe—what Cary Nelson calls the "replacement model" of hiring.* However, this is not what the doctors should be ordering. If the department attempts to replace Prof. Johnson, a specialist in, say, structural linguistics, with another of the same species through tradition or simply a failure of courage or imagination, it will have a hard time responding to its changing mission in a changing field. The department will be all the more constrained if it has shrunk by 10%, 15%, or even 20% since Prof. Johnson was hired—and such withering has been common over the past few decades, especially at public institutions.

Sometimes, of course, a new hire to replace the field expertise of a retiring colleague is precisely the right move. But to feel confident that it is, a department chair must open up a wide-ranging, blue-sky conversation that takes into consideration the current needs of the department, the strategic initiatives of the institution, new developments in the discipline, unmet desires of the department's students (as expressed in independent projects and requests for independent study courses and graduate seminars), and new areas of scholarship that might better respond to changing demographics within the student body and support the department's efforts to diversify its students. Such conversations are difficult, touching as they do on the expertise and (more sensitively) the "relevance" of the department's current faculty. There's no way to suggest that the department needs to make a new hire in an emerging area to catch up with the field without suggesting that at least some of the department faculty are somewhat behind the times. But there's also no way to move the department forward without such conversations. Sometimes they can pro-

*For discussion of the replacement model, see Stephen Watt, "What Is an 'Organization like the MLA'? From Gentleman's Club to Professional Association," *Workplace* 1 (1998): 27–35, https://louisville.edu/journal/workplace/features1/watt .html; Alyson Powell Key, "Colleges and Universities Adopt Cluster Hiring to Enhance Diversity among Faculty," Diversity in Research Jobs, March 30, 2020, https://www.diversityinresearch.careers/article/colleges-and-universities-adopt -cluster-hiring-to-enhance-diversity-among-faculty.

ductively be combined, in a department retreat, for instance, with a consideration of the department's current course offerings and major requirements.

Securing Permission to Hire

In the American college and university system, position control—that is, the authority to replace or create faculty positions—typically rests with the dean or provost. The faculty members who fill those positions reside in academic departments, of course, and department faculty have an understandable tendency to think of positions as "belonging" to the department: "We lost our medical anthropologist, so let's go out and find another one." But especially in an environment in which positions are in demand to represent new and emerging disciplines, programs, and departments and/or where changing enrollment patterns suggest a reallocation of faculty resources or where budget pressures restrict new hires, it's important to remember that in institutional terms, the position you've lost (through retirement, resignation, tenure denial, or even death) isn't "yours" and was never really yours: you had it on loan. And now, if you want it back, you'll have to make the case, supported with evidence (from a recent program review, from student enrollment data, from comparisons with departments at peer institutions), that you should have it again. (Such is obviously the case, even more starkly, when requesting a new position.)

Surely the biggest mistake academic departments make in arguing for new or replacement positions, whether that request goes through a faculty committee first or directly to the dean or provost, is taking a discipline's intellectual history, integrity, and importance—its own sense of itself—for granted. Which is to say that arguing for a position based on "what the discipline requires" instead of what the institution is trying to achieve is unlikely to win the day. In some professional and pre-professional disciplines with outside accreditation or licensure (architecture, for instance), professional accreditation all but guarantees certain kinds of faculty positions. But for most liberal arts disciplines, the specialties represented in a department are more fungible than we usually acknowledge within our disciplinary conversations, and you'll probably have to make the case using institutional rather than disciplinary logics to colleagues and administrators outside the department. It's not good enough to insist that a history department just isn't a history department without a paleographer to an audience that doesn't know what a paleographer is.

Better cases are made on two other grounds: demonstrated student demand and the planning documents of the department and the institution (the department's self-study and outside review; the college or university's strategic plan, vision statement, mission statement; etc.). Think of it as matchmaking: use your institution's articulated goals to frame or reframe your department's needs. Has your institution announced a commitment to admitting and supporting more first-generation students? If so, would it make sense in your request to replace a retiring nineteenth-century American historian with a historian of the American immigrant experience? If your introductory course in sociology is consistently overenrolled and a new faculty member could both teach that course and add an upper-division or graduate specialty that is not currently offered in the department, is in demand by students, and is allied with the institution's strategic plan, your department has a very strong case to make. If an institution is concerned about attracting more women and marginalized students in the STEM fields (science, technology, engineering, math), a physics department would be well advised to talk about strategies for identifying, recruiting, and retaining applicants from historically underrepresented groups. At many institutions, one avenue for this kind of appointment is a "target of opportunity" hire, an expedited process in which a midcareer or senior faculty member who is uniquely suited to meet your department's and institution's needs is pursued exclusively.

Allowing the institution's stated goals to influence a department's requests for faculty positions might appear cynical, and if you pursue it cynically, it will hardly help your department. If you succeed in securing a position that doesn't respond to the felt needs of the department's faculty and students, what have you really gained? At worst, you will have a new colleague who will struggle for enrollments, collegial connections, and intellectual community. The bottom line is that in requesting a position, your rhetorical task is not simply to make the case for what you and your colleagues want or need. The task is, rather, is to start with the felt needs of your department and then show how what you're asking for will help the college or university advance its larger strategic goals.

Most colleges and universities follow a process for considering hiring requests that can begin eighteen months or more before a new colleague would join the department. Different disciplines have different traditional hiring calendars based, at least in the past, on the dates of the discipline's big annual meeting(s), although these calendars have begun to soften in recent years as economic and sustainability considerations are inducing hiring departments to conduct early-stage interviewing via videoconferencing. But as a general rule, a department that wishes to bring on a new long-term (tenure-track or term) faculty member who will begin at the start of a new academic year will need to begin discussing the parameters of the position almost two years in advance (call it fall Year 0) and apply through the campus's process for permission to make the hire. That permission is typically granted in the spring or early summer. Advertising the position and first-round screening and interviews will, depending on the discipline, occur in the late summer or fall of Year 1 and final interviews (which are usually done on campus) take place in late fall Year 1 or early spring Year 2. The successful search will result in a hire that the dean's or provost's office formalizes during spring Year 2, and the new faculty member joins the department for the start of fall Year 2. Timelines for temporary (or visiting) positions are typically much shorter; requests to hire are perhaps due in the fall or early spring for appointments that begin the following fall.

Sometimes even when permission to hire is granted, it will come rather late. When a department advertises late in the season as a result, some involved in the process will argue that the search has been compromised because the best candidates will have already been hired by other institutions. Arguably, garnering only 125 instead of 150 applications for a position is hardly cause for despair, but the perception that a department might be settling for less than the best can haunt a new colleague who comes in under such a cloud—and the department that hires them—for years. In this circumstance, some will argue that the search should wait until the following year, perhaps with a request to the dean for a temporary faculty position to help with class coverage in the interim. Such a strategy is not without its risks. A postponed search may end up being canceled if the institution's budgetary picture sours, and some would argue that given recent shortages of college and university teaching positions, there are many good candidates from which a department might choose regardless of the timing of the search. As I'll discuss in more detail below, the search process for faculty is expensive and time consuming. The decision to "fail" a search or even postpone one is not to be taken lightly.

Beginning the Search Process

The dean or the provost has approved your department's request for a faculty position. What's next? The two next steps—writing the job ad and putting together the search committee—have a chicken-and-egg relationship. How can you choose a search committee before you've decided what you're searching for? But how can you write up an appropriate job advertisement without a search committee in place? Indeed, taking it back a step, how can a department present a persuasive position request to the administration without input and expertise from a group of department stakeholders? The answer, as we like to say in writing studies, is that the process is recursive: a general idea of what areas are needed in the department fuels a conversation with the faculty, which generates a position request, which in turn suggests a search committee, whose first order of business is to refine and publish the job ad.

How should you assemble the search committee? Some of this may be determined by your institution's rules governing searches. At my college, for instance, department chairs are always de facto search committee chairs. Such local regulations notwithstanding, the most important factor in putting together a search committee is just what you'd think: expertise. But remember, there are many kinds of relevant and useful expertise for a task like this one.

Most obviously, scholarly or artistic expertise is called for, and the faculty member (or members) whose disciplinary specialization overlaps with or is adjacent to the specialization you're trying to hire should under normal circumstances serve on the search committee and probably even chair it if possible. Such a colleague should be in a good position to assess the candidate's work in the field and to convey to other committee members and to the department as a whole the contribution the candidate's work is making or is likely to make to conversations in the field. The one instance in which this strategy can sometimes go wrong, however, is when a very senior member of the department is involved in the search for their replacement. Unless that colleague has been actively researching and thus kept up with the latest trends and conversations in their field and is unusually open minded, there is a danger that genuinely exciting new work produced by young scholars making their way through graduate school perhaps three or four decades later than they did will not be recognized for what it is. Usually senior scholars in the subfield are the best judges of new talent, but sometimes they're the worst. The temptation for the senior faculty member to tap a successor cut from the same cloth is almost beyond human powers to resist. For that reason, if a retiring colleague has the impulse to sit out the search for their replacement, you might be well advised to accept that parting gift.

Besides foregrounding disciplinary expertise, a search committee should include one or two members of the department known across campus for their skill in and dedication to teaching. Opportunities to observe job candidates in genuine (rather than highly artificial) teaching situations are quite rare, but good teachers have a knack for recognizing other good teachers, even in non-classroom interactions. Depending on institutional traditions and norms, one or more students may be asked to serve on a search committee. At my undergraduate institution, this participation is mandated (and even if it were not, it's hard to imagine hiring a faculty member here without robust student participation). My college also requires the participation of one faculty member from outside the hiring department—someone who is knowledgeable about and sympathetic to the goals of the department but who, because they're not a member of the department, may be able when appropriate to question familiar ways of doing things and bring new ideas to bear. In the early stages, your search committee will also meet with a designated diversity officer of the college or university. In some systems that person becomes a member of the search committee, but in almost any search process today, the committee will be required to describe their concrete efforts to recruit a diverse pool of candidates and outline the steps they have taken to protect equity throughout the process.

Despite your best efforts and the best counsel of your colleagues, faculty searches will almost always surface ideological and interpersonal tensions among the faculty, even in an outwardly harmonious department. And in deeply divided departments—they do exist, and count yourself lucky if this comes as news to you—faculty searches can be extraordinarily difficult to navigate successfully. If a search committee is perceived to be composed of faculty members of only one ideological stripe, the results of that committee's deliberations are liable to be viewed with suspicion (if not outright hostility) by members of the other camp. (These camps need not be ideological or methodological: they can be generational or split along lines of gender, and so forth.) On the other hand, if a department chair attempts to constitute a "balanced" committee with representatives of each warring faction, the result can be gridlock and the consequences can be very dire for job candidates.

I will never forget one especially traumatic early interview I endured as a candidate for a very desirable position. The interviewers in the suite at the conference hotel were an Eminent Professor in My Field, a Rather Less Famous Professor in My Field, and the completely silent, though smiling, department chair, a scholar entirely outside my field. My own intellectual commitments were much closer to those of the Eminent Professor than to those of the Rather Less Famous Professor, but because of the profound disagreement between the two of them, any answer that pleased one was sure to anger the other. The experience is best captured in a phrase a friend used to describe a similar encounter of their own: "I felt like they were there to play handball and I was the wall." This is, of course, not a dynamic that you're hoping to create, and as chair, you'll need to use all your experience and all your personal knowledge of your colleagues to put together a committee that can both help find the ideal candidate and treat candidates fairly.

The Job Ad

One of the first tasks for the newly constituted search committee is to revisit the position description the department has submitted to the administration for its approval and make sure that it works as the text of a job advertisement. It's a question of making sure the description communicates properly to its new audience. In your request for a faculty position, you were describing expertise in terms appropriate for faculty and administrators outside your field. When you run an advertisement, of course, you're trying to connect with fellow specialists and can afford to use field-specific language. (Indeed, a job ad that looked just like the position description submitted for administrative approval could risk giving job candidates the impression that your department doesn't know what it is doing.)

When I was in graduate school and beginning to look at ads for faculty positions, I noticed that one prestigious department had posted essentially the same ad for several years running, announcing "one or more" positions "at any rank" in "any field of British or American literature." That's a pretty wide net. Recalling the slogan of a contemporaneous ad run by the US Marine Corps, I thought of this as the "looking for a few good men" strategy. One doesn't, of course, want to describe a job opening so narrowly that few if any candidates would pass through its needle's eye. Ironically, though, I always suspected that the ad in question was not actually broad but sneaky-narrow: a ruse for running a backroom, old boys' network-style search that seemed to welcome all comers. Only members of the club would have recognized that there was a secret handshake.

The simple fact is that properly defining a faculty position is a tricky, Goldilocks-like balancing act: not too narrow, not too broad. Some faculty who have been involved for decades in recruitment and hiring swear by the open-door approach: "Let's keep the description broad and see what we get." And there's something to that. Part of what's exciting about a faculty search— beyond the prospect of gaining a colleague—is that while the ad tells the applicants what you're looking for, the applicants and their application materials equally show you what you've been looking for all along without quite knowing it. And broad position descriptions can help generate a diverse applicant pool. It's an insight that applies to positions both broadly and narrowly described: the best new scholarly and artistic work, the brightest new minds in the field, the most promising new teachers will take you by surprise and take your breath away and rewrite your sense of the rules about what great scholarship and creativity and teaching look like. A good chair will do what they can to keep their colleagues' minds open to the serendipity of the process.

But to some degree—sometimes to a degree that can damage department cohesion—a broad initial ad means you're just postponing a difficult conversation and a difficult decision until later in the hiring process. Later—when heels are dug in; when colleagues have fallen for candidates (or been alienated by them), have invested time and hearts and minds; and the stakes for everyone, both faculty and candidates, are significantly higher. Welcoming very different kinds of applications means that you're setting up for yourself and your colleagues on the search committee the very difficult task of measuring quite different candidates (in different fields, sometimes even at different career stages) against one another with little or no common ground for comparison. As another 1980s TV commercial memorably put it, "You can pay me now or pay me later." Pay now: it's much cheaper. Have the difficult, position-shaping conversation early in the process and do your colleagues and potential job applicants the courtesy of deciding (more or less) what you want before you invite applicants into the pool.

Overseeing the Campus Interview

Once the position has been approved, the search committee has been constituted, and the job ad has been published, the search is well under way. As chair, your role becomes largely a supporting one: to assist the committee as necessary (and function as a committee member if that's part of your role) but otherwise to stay out of their way. You come back into the picture in a significant way once the committee has narrowed the applicant pool to a short list of two to four finalists who will be brought to campus for interviews.*

---

*I know this is odd. I'm not discussing the screening interviews, or what used to be the disciplinary-conference interviews, and the conversation and

Ideally with the help of an able department administrator, as chair you will be responsible for making sure that candidates brought to campus are given ample opportunity to learn about your department, your students, your institution, and your community and given a chance, too, to demonstrate their abilities as thinkers and teachers and what they would contribute to your program. In the campus interviews I have overseen as chair, it seemed to me that three aspects of the visit in particular required my attention.

First, although not all your colleagues will intuitively see it this way, at this point in the process your focus should shift from primarily screening candidates to courting them. The "buyer's market" logic that may have animated early stages of the search still obtains, but if all goes well, you're going to attempt to recruit one of the handful of candidates you've brought to campus to join your department, and you want to make that prospect an appealing one. Yes, there's still screening to do; yes, if your department requires one, the research talk should garner tough (though fair) questions, and the sample class or teaching demonstration should be scrutinized carefully. But these candidates are now prospective colleagues. Help them imagine what it would be like to work alongside you and your colleagues and why they should want to come join your department, especially if they have other opportunities. The campus visit stage of the search is when the search committee and the department—and, although this is out of your direct control, the dean and/or provost and any other members of the campus community (including students) they meet with— should start to woo the prospective candidates. As chair, it's your job, in part, to mastermind the charm campaign. Indeed, I've been told—more than once, in fact—that a candidate accepted

decision-making that results in the short list. They're absolutely make-or-break for a successful search. They're also not under your authority as chair unless you happen to be chair of the search committee.

our job offer because they looked forward to working with me. And believe me, I'm not that charming.

Such "charm" can take many forms, depending on your institution, your location, the "personality" of your department, and your own personal style. For instance, because ground transportation in Southern California can be a nightmare, I try whenever possible to meet job candidates at the airport when they fly here. It's a personal touch, it doesn't cost me much, and I think it helps send a good message and set a good tone for the visit. (On the other hand, I try to keep arrangements for the return trip to the airport flexible. It's sometimes a mercy to allow a candidate who you're pretty certain will not be offered the job to have a bit of down time on their way back home. By the same token, I know of at least one case in which a hire was essentially cinched at the loading zone after a great campus visit and lively and frank conversation on the drive back to the airport.)

Depending on local norms, you may want to offer to drive a candidate through some of the neighborhoods around campus so they can imagine themself living there. Sometimes departments arrange a tour of homes conducted by a realtor, although these can come across as a bit aggressive and, of course, lack the personal touch of a tour with a potential colleague. Some departments make a point of hosting at least one of the candidate's dinners in the home of a faculty member, another "homey" touch, although at some institutions, this would seem a bit contrived. But give careful thought to what you and your colleagues can do to give finalists an authentic sense of what it would be like to work with you and live in your community.

The second and third areas of focus for me are much of a piece. I make it my jobs to ensure that demonstrations of both scholarship and teaching (which take different forms at different institutions) are fair to all the candidates and to give each the opportunity to appear at their best. For the research presentation, this includes providing candidates with very clear expectations in writing.

Depending on the discipline, this might include things like whether the department is expecting a talk from notes or a formal academic (conference-style) presentation; who will likely make up the audience, hence at what level the presentation should be pitched; the availability of audiovisual technology, and so forth. Just as importantly, the faculty and students who attend the presentation and who will be part of the hiring decision need to know what instructions were given to the candidate so they're assessing the performance according to appropriate criteria.

In my experience, the teaching demonstration—which might take the form of a sample class, a teaching presentation, or some other format—can go wrong in myriad ways and/or fail to provide much useful information to the search committee about the candidate's teaching ability or potential. A talk about the candidate's teaching experience and teaching philosophy isn't really teaching, is it? There are some terrible teachers out there who can rattle off a pretty polished pitch about their teaching philosophy. What about when a candidate takes over a session of a faculty colleague's class? It can be difficult to simply slip into an ongoing semester-long conversation and an established group dynamic as an outsider. What about asking the candidate to teach a stand-alone "demonstration" class to students the department recruits? This is better, perhaps, although if the class is expected to include discussion, students may be reluctant to participate, since those conversational rhythms take some time to develop, certainly longer than a single class period. That said, there is valuable information to be gleaned from the ways prospective colleagues deal with these challenges, and here, as with the research presentation, candidates must be given uniform instructions about the task that are also shared with those evaluating the performance.

What I've written to this point imagines a situation in which the hiring department is able to bring a short list of candidates to campus. Call me old fashioned, but I still think this is the best way to assess candidates' potential as future colleagues, teachers, and scholars. It goes without saying, I hope, that all expenses for such visits must be borne by the hiring department. Ideally, all the major expenses (airfare, lodging, meals) are paid in advance by the department and the candidate pays out of pocket only for incidentals, which are quickly reimbursed. Over the past two hiring seasons, however, in part because of restrictions on travel and in-person meetings during the pandemic, many institutions have chosen to conduct this final stage of interviewing virtually. This practice is likely to persist into the future. It's far less expensive, both in terms of institutional budgets and faculty time and energy, and virtual meetings are far easier to schedule. And in the case of non-tenure-track faculty searches, an institution is much less likely to budget for an on-campus interview stage. If it's at all possible to meet your finalists in person and let them see your campus, meet your students and colleagues, and experience the community, well, there's simply no substitute. As chair, to the extent that you're able, you should argue that the time and expense are worthwhile because getting this decision wrong is so costly.

But if you'll be making your final decision based purely on video interaction, the past few years have taught us some valuable lessons about how to make such interviews equitable and ensure that your search committee emerges with the information they need to make a decision. By now, most of us have some level of familiarity with platforms like Zoom. Beyond the normal best practices for creating a level playing field for candidates (making sure that similar questions are asked of each candidate, appointing someone to moderate the interview), perhaps the most important thing you can do is to make sure you have a backup plan if the technology fails. (Make sure, for instance, that the candidates have your cell phone number and that you have theirs.) For more information on virtual interview best practices, the guidelines put together by the University of Maryland, Baltimore County, are very good.*

*"COVID19 Virtual Faculty Interviewing Best Practices," UMBC Faculty Diversity, March 30, 2020, https://facultydiversity.umbc.edu/covid19-virtual-faculty-interviewing-best-practices/.

Selection and Job Offer

At most institutions, once a department has decided who they would like to hire, the process moves to the dean's office. A department makes its choice (subject to administrative approval), but the unit responsible for the salary works out the details of the offer and contract. Depending on the structure at your institution, this can create an exciting opportunity for you as the chair. You're now simply the candidate's advocate; you can now talk candidly with them about how to negotiate for what they need to make the position work for them, and you may also be in a position to intercede with the dean on their behalf. That said, I've always found this moment in the search to be very stressful. My colleagues and I have decided who we want, but I have few if any levers to make that hire happen and have to leave the negotiating to my dean, who doesn't know the candidate or the department and its needs as well as I do. This is one of many times when it pays to have built up a good working relationship with your dean.

But I've skipped a step, of course. How does a department determine its rankings of the finalists who have come to campus? In some happy circumstances, the choice is crystal clear: there is unanimity or near-unanimity among department faculty (and students, if they have a role in the selection) and the dean is happy to assent to the department's recommendation. Happy searches, to paraphrase Tolstoy, are all alike, but every unhappy search is unhappy in its own way. We choose our new colleagues by committee, as we ought, but sometimes those choices bear the marks of decision by committee: we choose the best candidate for the position that everyone involved can agree on. In some cases, that procedure will favor the genial but safe candidate, promoting the (imagined) "good colleague" over the distinguished teacher and/ or scholar.

It would be unjust to call such appointments a compromise, since a faculty position in any reputable academic department in the country will receive more outstanding curriculum vitae than you can shake a stick at. Indeed, one of the more uncomfortable consequences of the depressed job market of the past two decades is that search committee members and even committee and department chairs often lack the scholarly credentials of the candidates they are interviewing (and rejecting) for entry-level jobs. But too often, committees fail to make their offer to the best-qualified candidate from a frighteningly accomplished and competitive pool of applicants.

Some years ago, when a close friend of mine was informally offered their first tenure-track job in one of the nation's finest English departments, the senior professor in their field told them at the conclusion of the Modern Language Association's convention, "We've now spoken to all the best young scholars in the field in the country, and you're clearly the best." This department was confident that it had identified that year's young star in their field, and it hired them. It sounds simple, but the process rarely works that way. For all but the handful of best departments in the country, several extraneous factors too often prevent us from accomplishing what we've set out to do. Among them are the fear that the "best person" won't come or won't stay: they're too good for us, we fear, and rather than letting them tell us so (by accepting another position or leaving us later for another job), we'll not ask them. Far too often, in my experience, when we say "the best person," we really mean "the best person who we're confident will come and stay."

Hiring the best person always involves the risk that they will leave at some point. I'd go so far as to argue that having colleagues leave for better jobs is evidence that a department has hired well. In any given year, Harvard might hire the best Shakespearean on the market, only to have them leave for Duke five years later. Yale may make an offer to the season's hot young molecular biologist, only to have them turn them down for a job at Wisconsin. Yet they risk it.

Some years ago, the department I was chairing persuaded the most promising young scholar in their field (in my judgment) to come join our faculty. A few short years later, they left us for a position elsewhere, and it was without a doubt a better position for them given the strengths of the department they joined. I was personally disappointed to lose such a smart and energetic colleague but professionally proud to have picked them from a crowded field of applicants and to have persuaded them to come to my department. We did well to hire them, and our department was the richer during the time they were with us and better as a result of their having spent time with us. Some would say that losing a faculty member to another institution—whether 3, 10, or 20 years after hiring them—means that the hire was a failure. Certainly faculty hires are expensive and the resources invested in identifying, hiring, and mentoring a new faculty member are significant. But I would always choose to see such a transition as a measure of our success: we were able to identify a colleague on an upward professional arc and were able to support them in a way that furthered their career. As difficult (and expensive) as faculty turnover is, it's probably inevitable if you're doing your job well.

One especially unattractive version of this problem involves being used by a midcareer or senior professor who has no real interest in joining your department but who requires your expression of interest to improve their position at their home institution or at other institutions who are courting them. It's deeply embarrassing to find out that the cute guy asked you to the dance only so that his partner would see the two of you there together and be jealous. At the same time, it is a tenacious fact of most university salary systems that an outside offer is just about the only leverage a faculty member has to improve their salary. I'll leave it to the *Chronicle of Higher Education*'s Ms. Mentor or the *New York Times Magazine*'s The Ethicist to parse the moral implications of such duplicitous job searches. Without contradicting my previous observations, it's safe to say that often these applications in search of a counteroffer can be detected by a search committee that is not susceptible to the applicant's flattery. The psychology department at my college is very good, but if Steven Pinker applied for a job here, they'd be right to be suspicious. He'd better have a pretty good story.

The "Failed Search" and Other Search Failures

Faculty searches fail for many other reasons. Sometimes all of the finalists are disappointing during their campus interviews and sometimes the one or two who do impress have also impressed others and accept offers from other institutions or, if they already have a permanent position, choose to remain where they are. Sometimes members of a department may feel threatened by the addition of a genuinely talented and ambitious young faculty member (someone who will raise the bar), fearing, whether consciously or subconsciously, that the candidate's productivity will make them look bad. Or the complicated set of circumstances and negotiations surrounding spousal or partner hires may result in gridlock. I even know of a case in which the clear-cut top candidate for a job was passed over because their name was too similar to that of an already tenured member of the department. (No, I'm not making this up.)

These and other problems make for great stories, and the novelists Richard Russo, David Lodge, Jane Smiley, and others have written them. But the darker side of faculty hiring is that we risk wasting enormous economic, intellectual, administrative, emotional, and interpersonal resources in the process of finding new colleagues. My rough calculations suggest that when one factors in the cost of advertising a position; the time search committee members, support staff, and college and university administrators spend reviewing letters of application, curricula vitae, letters of recommendation, and writing samples; sending the search committee to a national conference for initial screening (in the cases where this is still done); and bringing finalists to the campus for interviews, the price of conducting a tenure-track search is, at least outside professional schools, about the same as the first-year salary of that new faculty member.

Despite that significant expenditure of human and economic capital, most academics have received no formal training in how to conduct a faculty search. Given that (as one wag said) at any moment half the professoriate is out trying to hire the other half, it's shocking that we spend so little time or money learning how to do it well. No corporation would allow such waste. In my era, PhD students in my graduate department spent an average of 7.33 years mastering the tools of literary and cultural research, but in the 30-plus years since then, I have spent only a handful of hours in formal training in the best practices for academic hiring, even in my roles as associate dean and department chair.

It's not just scarce institutional resources that we waste when we hire badly, as important as that problem is. Every search to fill an academic position, especially at the entry level, puts at least a handful of vulnerable people through a long, demanding, and often demoralizing process. The professoriate is to some extent what Stephen Dedalus (in James Joyce's *A Portrait of the Artist as a Young Man*) called Ireland: the old sow that eats her farrow (litter). One of my colleagues in graduate school, having persevered until the very end of a long search and been invited to campus for a three-day visit, returned home and heard nothing from the hiring department for six weeks. When they finally screwed up their courage and phoned the department chair, the department secretary curtly told them that the position had gone to someone else. Those we damage today in our inept searches will, if they somehow survive and enter the academy, almost certainly go on to damage the next generation in their turn. As chair, make it your responsibility to provide semifinalists as much information as you can regarding their standing in the search and your institution's timetable.

Hiring Adjunct Faculty

The process I've just outlined is the maximalist approach to hiring, and it's based on best practices that have evolved around tenure-track searches. But even in departments that still hire faculty into tenure lines, a portion (likely a growing portion) of the teaching is done by non-tenure-track faculty, and the hiring process for these positions is often much simpler. In some cases, as for instance when adding sections of a general education course, a chair will make these appointments on their own or with the help of one or two colleagues who volunteer to help review applications and interview candidates. Often these appointments are made without an on-campus interview. As a result, those who participate in the screening process must be especially alert for evidence of teaching experience and good teaching evaluations, in the form of a letter of recommendation that focuses on the candidate's teaching, for instance.

Because adjunct faculty can be hired without the same degree of department participation, a chair must take extra steps to ensure that the new hire both has a peer group to connect with and receives appropriate mentoring and support for their professional development. Both of these topics will be addressed in later chapters.

"Something might be gaining on you"

It's worth remembering that in hiring new faculty members to join our departments, we ask ourselves and our colleagues to do a difficult thing: identify and hire scholars and teachers who will make the rest of us look bad. Here the lines from Andrew Marvell's "To His Coy Mistress" are relevant:

> But at my back I always hear
> Time's wingéd chariot hurrying near;
> And yonder all before us lie
> Deserts of vast eternity.

Our junior colleagues represent the hope that springs eternal: their energy and promise can potentially enhance our departments, our institutions, and our disciplines. But they also drive time's wingéd chariot. The famous Negro League pitcher Satchel Paige advised, "Don't look back. Something might be gaining on you," and the new colleagues we work so hard to find and woo are precisely those who are gaining on us, pushing us one step closer to those "deserts of vast eternity."

Hiring well, then, fundamentally contradicts human nature. Perhaps we shouldn't be surprised that sometimes the process goes wrong but instead celebrate when we get it right. According to a once-current saying in Silicon Valley, "The A team hires the A team; the B team hires the C team." If we are to get it right more often than we currently do, we're going to have to put our heads together and become smarter and better than any of us is on our own. And as department chair, that's your job: you're the one faculty member who is responsible for preserving the integrity of the process over personal likes and dislikes. You're not hiring a friend or even a colleague (although with luck, the new hire may turn out to be one or both); you're hiring the future of your department.

Chapter 2

Mentoring Faculty

Faculty development—mentoring faculty, supporting their professional and personal aspirations, mobilizing the resources at your command to facilitate their professional growth—is some of the most rewarding work a department chair gets to do. In choosing to accept the role of chair, you accept (if only tacitly) the responsibility to put others' needs before your own, at least for a season; but when you celebrate various accomplishments with colleagues and recognize that you have played a role in making them possible, that tradeoff begins to make sense.

To open this chapter, let's loop back for a moment to the closing pages of chapter 1. For a department chair, faculty mentoring begins the moment you welcome a candidate to campus for an interview (if not during the screening interview that precedes it). To the extent that mentoring is intentional modeling, you started mentoring your new colleague when you began to treat them as a prospective colleague by expressing interest in their research, paying close attention to their teaching, listening as they laid out future plans and dreams. But the mentoring that can happen with a job candidate is severely limited. Some of the feedback they will receive from your colleagues on the research presentation might prove useful as the project goes forward, but it's unlikely that you'll provide any substantive criticism of their teaching demonstration, for instance. Then too, you don't yet have a real, durable relationship with the candidate; the day or two of their campus visit may be the last time you ever work together. For these reasons, the mentoring that happens before hiring is primarily passive. It consists of modeling the way you and your colleagues live your professional lives, both together and separately, and providing a (hopefully appealing) picture of what it would be like to join your department.

Mentoring a New Faculty Colleague through the Transition

After you've made a new hire and gained a new colleague, your primary responsibility to them as their chair is to do everything within your power to ensure their success, both on the institution's terms and on their own. For the sake of being comprehensive, I will assume that the faculty member has been hired on the tenure track, but much if not all of the advice is equally applicable to faculty members hired for term or contract positions without the possibility of tenure, even if the stages and inflection points of such a career path are somewhat different. (The kinds of support senior faculty desire, on the other hand, are quite distinct, and I'll address them at the end of this chapter.)

Most institutions will offer (if not require) some kind of orientation process for new faculty hires before the start of the first instructional term. Topics range from the prosaic (getting a faculty ID, signing up for benefits) to the profound, including the tenure and promotion expectations and procedures of the institution. As part of the orientation process, many institutions will assign a faculty mentor. This person is someone your new colleague can share challenges with, ask questions of, and seek advice from in a nonjudgmental, nonthreatening environment. Precisely because the advice is meant to be formative rather than evaluative, such mentors are usually selected from outside the new faculty member's home department. Ideally, this will be an allied department but one whose faculty will not be involved, at least in the earliest round, in the evaluation for tenure and promotion. A new computer science faculty member may be assigned a mentor from mathematics; an assistant professor of sociology may be mentored by a senior faculty member of the economics department. Usually the new colleague is paired with someone of the same gender because some of the issues and pressures that new faculty face are gender specific.

Whatever your institution's programming for new faculty is, a new colleague's last couple of weeks before the start of classes are going to be given over to macro, largely nonprofessional considerations: working out campus parking; trying to learn the names of all their new departmental faculty colleagues and administrative staff; figuring out where to get dry cleaning done; memorizing an office number, an email address, passwords, and a new phone number; getting a laboratory up and running. As department chair, you may have some role to play in these early days. At the very least, treating your new colleague to lunch will mean that they've learned one decent place to eat, whether on campus or off. While they'll likely be eager to resume the work that led to their dissertation or perhaps pursue new avenues of research or creative work branching off from it, especially at an institution with research expectations, their biggest transition coming from graduate school will be to the volume and type of teaching they're called upon to do as a full-time faculty member. Many institutions recognize this steep learning curve into college teaching by suggesting, whether formally or informally, that new faculty members focus on their adjustment to teaching and to the institution and its students, putting research and creative activity on the back burner for a semester or two.

The first, most urgent area for professional growth, then, and the area in which your new faculty colleague will most immediately benefit from mentoring, is teaching. Institutional traditions and practices differ on this point, but an early, informal—and crucially, undocumented (or at least unarchived)—visit to observe one or more class sessions can help put things on the right footing early on. As chair, you need not be the observer; indeed, it's probably best that you're not. For even though in some institutions a department chair has very little real power, you are perceived as the "boss"—albeit with scare quotes—and if you're still in the chair's position in five years' time, you'll be running your colleague's tenure review. While you may say that the observation will be purely formative and strictly for the colleague's benefit, that's going to be hard for a new hire to believe. See whether you can have an unthreatening junior colleague (and one whose teaching is going well) visit the course instead. Unless your institution's policies mandate an early, on-the-record class visitation, it's best if the new colleague invites the visitor rather than the visitor inviting themself. A "you visit mine and I'll visit yours" arrangement in which your new colleague is both seen teaching and sees how others approach it is even better. It might be helpful to have the new faculty member's institutionally assigned mentor observe their teaching too, but because norms and best practices in teaching can vary widely across disciplines, someone from your own department needs to be part of the feedback loop. Observations and advice should be supportive and should be shared only with the new colleague; no written record should be kept. This is information to be used solely for the new colleague to improve their teaching, not for purposes of departmental or institutional evaluation, and it should not be part of any institutional paper trail.

Beyond the adjustment to full-time teaching, there's another key transition for a new faculty member to make, and as their chair and their champion, you may be best positioned to help them make it. Your new colleague is coming to you either fresh from graduate school or from another teaching position, which is to say, a different academic culture from the one they now find themself in. Over time, through trial and error, they'll learn what's distinctive about their new institution and what they need to do differently, but some of us are better at learning from experience than others, and the "error" piece of "trial and error" can have lasting consequences for a probationary faculty member. Sure, some of us finish our graduate training and land at institutions very much like the one that trained us, but that's the rare exception. Instead, most of us need to leave grad school (or that last job) behind and adjust to a new reality.

Think back to when you came to the department you now chair, whether it was your first job or your fourth. What's different about the way your department organizes itself, makes decisions, thinks about seniority, prioritizes teaching and research and service, and thinks about work-life balance? What are the important events in the recent history of the department that help explain these things? What about the institution itself: What is its mission statement? How does it affect the day-to-day operations of the place? What does the mission statement communicate about what the institution expects of its faculty and staff? Who does the institution identify as its peers and what does that say about where it's trying to go? And what are your students like? What are their expectations—and the institution's—regarding faculty members' availability? What about simple (but sometimes nontrivial) things such as how faculty are expected to dress for class?

What we're talking about here is something like an ethnography of your department, your college or university, and your students, and you are the native informant for your new faculty colleague. At that first lunch you invite them out to, make this one of the topics of conversation: think of it as "things I wish I'd known about this place when I arrived." That might sound like the setup to a long list of complaints and grievances, but it needn't be. If I were giving it today to a new colleague at my institution, it certainly wouldn't be. Rather, I'd be pointing out the opportunities that present themselves in this new place and how your new colleague might really make their mark, how they might contribute to making the department a place where they love working.

Formal Pre-tenure Evaluations

In addition to the informal mentoring suggested above, your institution will also have in place a system of mandatory faculty evaluations that it will be your duty as chair to oversee. There are a few different models in place, but a typical system and time-table will include a review at or near the end of the first year, another during or at the close of the third year, and the tenure review, which normally happens during the sixth year. In many systems, the pre-tenure contracts are written around these reviews: a new hire comes in with a one-year contract, which is renewed for two years after a satisfactory first-year review, is renewed for a further three years after the third-year review, and then is either made permanent after a successful tenure review or concluded with a final one-year contract in the case of tenure denial. (In most systems, the review for tenure is coupled with the review for promotion to associate professor, although some institutions allow the granting of tenure without the conferral of promotion and some allow promotion to associate professor without or even before the awarding of tenure.)

I have come to think of the first-year review as a kind of fail-safe—a low-stakes check-in to make sure nothing is misfiring badly, especially regarding teaching. In my current institution, the first-year review, at least as it's implemented in my department, seeks to ensure that the adjustment to teaching is going well and provide resources for an early correction if necessary—and that's really about it. No department or college service is expected; no new faculty member at my institution is given a committee assignment in their first year. And if a new faculty member has been able to advance their research or creative work in the first year, however incrementally, that's all to the good and would be celebrated in the review, but there's no expectation of research productivity in that first year. Further—and although this might vary by institution, I've not yet heard of any exceptions—no faculty member would be dismissed based on the results of a first-year review, unless for some type of gross misconduct.

The third-year review is more diagnostic. Given the performance of the first three years in the three key areas of faculty responsibility (teaching, research and/or creative activity, and service), is the faculty member on track to achieve tenure and promotion when the tenure review comes around? At institutions fortunate enough to have some form of junior research leave, the third-year review sometimes also functions as an application for that leave, which is granted contingent upon successful completion of the review. Again, practices vary, but at my institution, the first-year review is written by the chair in consultation with department faculty and is rather brief (a single-spaced page, perhaps running onto a second). The third-year review, by contrast, includes input from three anonymous outside reviewers and is drafted by a subcommittee of the department. At this stage, all three areas of faculty responsibility are assessed. By this point, the candidate should be starting to participate in departmental and/or institutional service of some kind. As chair, you have the ability to help your colleague aim for an appropriate service assignment to a committee that does meaningful (but not onerous) work. And while it is rare, at some institutions, the contract of a faculty member can be terminated if their performance at the third-year review indicates severe deficits in one or more areas of responsibility.

In the assessment of teaching, student evaluations and peer observations should paint a picture of a teacher who is developing an effective personal style and is connecting with their students. If teaching seems to be progressing at an unacceptably slow pace, there may be institutional resources that can be brought into play. The department, college, or university may have "master teachers" or a teaching and learning center the faculty member can be encouraged to work with. Activities can include (more) peer observation (both observation of the less experienced teacher by the more senior and vice versa) and viewing and dissecting recorded class sessions, again with an experienced teacher. If departmental or institutional resources allow, the chair may be able to identify external workshops, seminars, or conferences that focus on teaching—whether postsecondary teaching broadly or teaching in the discipline more specifically—and offer to send the faculty member.

Other support that a chair can provide a junior colleague comes in the form of teaching assignments. Some new faculty members leap at the chance to develop and teach new courses at every opportunity. Some departments, eager to attract new students and develop new areas of the curriculum, are happy to let them. And for a successful, seemingly "naturally" gifted teacher, this might be the right thing to do, especially if those new courses align with their evolving research interests and provide opportunities for synergy between teaching and scholarship. But at most institutions with any kind of research expectation for tenure, no amount of teaching of new courses will make up for a lack of research productivity at the point of the tenure review. Many chairs advise their new faculty to teach a uniform set of courses for the first two or three years and learn to teach them really well, emphasizing quality over quantity. At all institutions, whether research oriented, teaching oriented, or some middle ground between the two, tenure and promotion require a tricky balancing act. As chair, it's your job to help your junior colleague figure out the appropriate balance—"charting a path of efficiency and growth," as my colleague Dan O'Leary puts it.

At most institutions, whether or not they offer tenure-track faculty a junior research leave, there's often a piece missing in the support the institution offers tenure-track faculty—and that is some kind of low-stakes, informal check-in between the third-year and tenure reviews. I became especially aware of this when I served on a college-wide committee that reviews tenure and promotion cases. At my institution, junior leave (taken in the fourth tenure-track year) is applied for early in the third year and is granted to all who pass that review. When I was reviewing dossiers three years later for tenure review on the college committee, though, I became concerned about faculty who were reviewed early in their third year, sent off to work in relative isolation in the fourth, and then were essentially not on the college's radar again until the tenure review, when it was too late to make any necessary corrections. On the college-wide committee, I read leave applications that outlined what were (for instance) clearly unrealistic book projects, then three years later read about the collapse of those plans in the tenure research statement. What a waste that the institution didn't have a way to connect with the faculty member after that fourth-year leave, when there was still time to right the ship.

As department chair, you may have some supportive and non-threatening ways to make that check-in to make sure that your junior colleague carries momentum forward after the third-year review and is on track to clear the bar for tenure. In my department, we've created an optional outside scholarly review of book manuscripts of junior faculty before they submit them to a scholarly press; this happens before the tenure review. It's not an inexpensive proposition, but there are other low- or no-cost interventions that a chair might make in order to support their junior colleagues. At the very least, an informal conversation sometime in the fourth year will suggest your continued commitment to their success and your willingness to help.

Tenure and Promotion Review

Tenure is the crown jewel of the American higher education system, the brass ring, as a friend outside academia once described it to me. In its current form, tenure dates to the 1940 "Statement of Principles on Academic Freedom and Tenure" formulated by the American Association of University Professors in conjunction with the Association of American Colleges and Universities. The dual subjects in the document's title suggest the relationship between them: tenure exists in order to protect academic freedom so American college and university faculty members may teach and pursue their research without fear of undue influence or pressure. It represents a level of job security practically unparalleled in other forms of employment. Once a faculty member has been awarded tenure, they can be fired only for cause or if the institution declares financial exigency. Such dismissals are very rare.

In return for such a level of job security, the process for attaining tenure is rigorous, and nearly every specific can vary from one institution to another. The path to tenure at a research university typically spans six to seven years, while at some two-year colleges, the process lasts just three. Some departments at some institutions require two scholarly books to meet the research standard (or in disciplines in which books are not the norm, an equivalent number of well-placed articles or papers, citations, major grants, and grant applications). In some others where teaching is weighted more heavily, a single journal article or even conference presentation may suffice. Some colleges will expect evidence of extraordinary teaching and mentoring of students, while some larger research-intensive institutions will be satisfied with evidence of competent and responsible teaching. At my institution, we have added criteria that focus on creating an inclusive classroom environment to our tenure and promotion standards. And so on. This variability in every aspect of the process makes it difficult to generalize about a chair's role in supporting junior faculty through it. But some strategies and principles apply across different institutional types and values.

If all this sounds a bit vague—especially with regard to a high-stakes review—departmental and institutional standards can be equally, frustratingly, so. To some extent this is by design. While documents outlining tenure requirements suggest minimum requirements in teaching, research, and service, they typically soften the focus a bit when it comes to details, allowing review committees, deans, provosts, presidents, and boards of trustees the discretion to evaluate a case "holistically" (or so the argument goes). For instance, what does "excellent" or "outstanding" or even "good" teaching look like in practice? How is it assessed—with student course evaluations, faculty observation, teaching awards, student and alumni letters? How are different teaching styles, whether personal or discipline-based, accounted for? How much service is enough, and where (department, institution, profession) should the faculty member's service efforts be focused? And assessing research productivity is not a simple matter of bean counting: quality should matter as much or more than quantity but is arguably harder to measure, or at least to agree upon. A penumbra of uncertainty surrounds each of the criteria for tenure.

That notwithstanding, as soon as a junior colleague is hired, you should provide them with any written departmental, college, and/or university standards regarding tenure and promotion. When it comes to the fine art of interpreting them—of trying to apply those standards to the teaching, service, and scholarship of your colleague—you're in as good a position as anyone to predict how a future tenure and promotion committee will regard the dossier. Although you will probably want to conceal identities for the sake of privacy, recent cases at your institution will give you some idea of how the standards are being interpreted. While past cases provide no solid precedent because standards are living and evolving, they should give you a good idea. All of which is to say, when it comes to assessing the tenure dossier as it's coming together, you're well positioned as chair to comment and advise, while of course you aren't in any position to make predictions.

What is the chair's role in tenure review? In order to advocate for the case, of course, a chair must be convinced that tenure has been earned. In all the systems I'm familiar with, the chair of a department has at least their own independent vote on the case as a member of the department faculty. In some processes, the chair has instead—or in addition—a separate chair review of the case. Normally, a tenure case proceeds through a series of reviews, starting with the local—a recommendation by the home department, which may be based on the recommendation of a subcommittee of the department—and moving through upper layers of the institution's administrative structure. This may include one or all of the following levels in a university organized by colleges: review by the tenure candidate's college in a college-level personnel committee; review of that committee's recommendation by a dean; review of the college's and/or dean's recommendation by a university-wide tenure and promotion committee, whose report typically goes to a provost; review by the provost; review by the president; review by a system-wide chancellor; and review and ratification by an institution's board of trustees.

But no matter how elaborate an institution's process or how many levels of review it may entail, it all starts with the home department, and as chair, it's your job to ensure that the process is carried out fairly and responsibly and that the candidate's credentials and performance as a teacher and scholar are judged as dispassionately as possible by their department colleagues. A tenure review can be unfair in two different directions, by being strongly biased for or strongly biased against a faculty member. In a small department especially and in those characterized by a high teaching load, faculty colleagues have a great deal of interaction. Sometimes that endears us to one another and sometimes it has quite the opposite effect. As chair, it is your job to ensure that personal likes and dislikes are kept out of the personnel process—and that includes your own personal, nonprofessional impressions of a faculty colleague.

I've drifted into talking a bit about personnel evaluation and the tenure process itself. What does it mean to mentor a tenure-track faculty member and help them through the process? If the tenure review is conducted in the sixth year, then (depending on the length of your term as chair) you've already committed up to five years to mentoring this colleague. You've supported them with resources to improve their teaching and you've involved them in meaningful service work, work that is likely to have a real impact and through which they're likely to meet important senior colleagues across the institution and come to the attention of deans and the provost. At the same time, you've protected them from high-demand, low-impact service assignments. The junior faculty I've mentored over the years have always known that I'd be their heavy; if they were asked to join a working group or campus committee, give a talk to a community group, and so forth, they knew they could say that they'd really like to but their chair wouldn't let them. Sometimes being chair means being the fall guy: get used to it.

Research and/or creative activity, the third area for tenure and promotion, can be the most difficult area for a chair to provide knowledgeable mentorship in for a number of reasons. To begin with, your specialty within your discipline is likely different from that of your faculty colleague. Some disciplinary conversations and norms cut across specializations, but very specific advice about fruitful research paths, meaningful conferences to attend, and rigorous journals to publish in can be quite area-specific. Also, while colleagues' teaching and campus service are public and visible to members of the campus community, scholarship and creative work can in some cases be carried out rather privately so that it's difficult for a chair to know in advance of publication just what kind of progress is being made. To the degree possible, though—to the degree that you can engage with their work with real understanding and provide feedback and advice that your tenure-track department colleagues find meaningful—you should be reading their research, providing comments, and highlighting for them any relevant funding opportunities you become aware of. Encourage your junior colleagues to apply to and attend the most important conferences and meetings in their field and help them figure out how to fund their attendance. Chairs should also be nominating junior colleagues for any award, prize, or recognition in their field as they become aware of these opportunities.

For this kind of mentoring to be experienced as meaningful, faculty members must respect their chair as a scholar or creator in their own right who has gone through the credentialing process successfully, just as the tenure-track colleague is now attempting to do. For this reason, I've always thought it best that department chairs be selected from faculty who are respected for both their teaching and their research. For the same reason, it's a good idea, when local conditions allow, to choose a full professor to chair the department—someone who has successfully gone through all the reviews their colleagues will be facing, who has some credibility as a guide through those processes, and whose support at the college and university levels will carry more weight.

Mentoring beyond Tenure

In a way that subhead is misleading, for all good mentoring should be mentoring beyond tenure—which is to say, mentoring that acknowledges that tenure is not the ultimate goal. At the top of the chapter, I suggested that in your mentoring role, your job as chair is to ensure the success of your faculty colleagues both on the institution's terms and on their own. If you're coaching them only on how to win tenure, there's a danger that you're not listening to what success would look like for them. For many, perhaps, it is precisely tenure: nothing more and surely nothing less. But too often I've seen ambitious faculty members join a department burning white hot, ready to set the field on fire, but by the time they get tenure, if indeed they do, their big dreams have been constrained by the size and shape of the containers the institution provides. The tenure standards at your institution, whether quite specific or (far more common) frustratingly vague, set the minimum required for continued employment. These standards must be met, of course. But sometimes setting tenure as the end goal rather than an interim bar to be cleared means that faculty members are encouraged, if only implicitly, to sell themselves and their work short—to realize short- or medium-term gains that can be produced for a tenure dossier instead of making big, ambitious bets on truly surprising new work.

I'm being vague because the individual circumstances of disciplines, departments, institutions, and scholars vary so widely. Let me suggest just one concrete example from my field before moving on. In some English departments, a scholarly monograph (and sometimes more) is required for tenure; in others, a handful of journal articles will suffice. A junior scholar might enter a hypothetical English department planning to revise their dissertation into an important monograph, but if by the end of the fourth year or so that manuscript isn't yet in publishable form, they're faced with a decision. Should they bet on the monograph, continue to put the time into revision, and trust that a positive publication decision will be forthcoming before the tenure vote is taken? Or should they instead set the book project aside because of time constraints and instead submit a few articles? There's no obviously right strategy here, except that any gambit that cost your colleague their job was probably, in retrospect, the wrong one.

But it's important to recognize in this example that by abandoning the manuscript and salvaging some articles, your colleague has paid a price. They're now far less likely to be able to move to a more attractive position at another institution, one that has more demanding research standards, for instance, because they "sold short." In the discipline of English, at least, scholarly monographs for the most part attract far more attention and prestige than journal articles do. In the STEM fields, the consequences of the wrong decision most often are directly tied to whether a research project flourishes or withers. A chair might have valuable advice to give regarding hard decisions about whether to "fish or cut bait." All of this to say that there are costs involved in either decision and your job as chair is just to make sure, to the degree you're able, that your junior colleague is aware of them all and is making their decision based on what's best for their career and not just for their prospects at your institution.

For associate professors working toward a next promotion or full professors trying to identify a next phase in their careers, the timelines can be longer and the pressures more diffuse than for those on the tenure clock. Because colleagues in this group should have established healthy extramural support networks by this phase of their career, the specific advice of a department chair becomes less critical, especially as it pertains to research and scholarly activity. Since the timing of a review for promotion to full professor is at the discretion of the faculty member (barring possible requirements regarding minimum time in rank), one useful kind of feedback a chair can provide is encouragement when it's time to "go up": when the record of teaching and service and the body of research or creative activity has cleared the bar for promotion. In giving such advice, a chair can only give their own view, albeit one that is informed by experience in the department and the institution. Promotion is not a chair's prerogative, of course, so their opinion about whether or not the case is a strong one is necessarily subjective. In some systems, a chair or another faculty colleague can (and in other systems must) nominate a colleague for promotion. In that context, you may be able to encourage a colleague who has lost confidence in their work and needs a friendly nudge to move forward.

Mentoring Your Elders and Betters

For more senior colleagues who have already been promoted to full professor, a chair's role is only to make sure that the conditions of their work continue to provide professional and personal fulfilment. Perhaps a senior colleague has developed an interest in a new area of research and teaching and could use your help in finding opportunities to hone new skills or create a place in the curriculum to teach a new passion. Perhaps they instead feel the pull to academic leadership and could use your help in exploring opportunities. Perhaps, indeed, the next professional step for a senior colleague is to chair your department and you can have a hand in encouraging and mentoring them.

One circumstance that you're likely to face as chair but over which you can have very little influence is the senior colleague who in the eyes of their students and colleagues has ceased to be an asset and should consider retirement. Congress abolished mandatory retirement in 1986; that legislation grew out of the Age Discrimination in Employment Act of 1967, which also made it illegal for an employer or anyone (like a department chair) who can be seen to be representing the interests of the employer to suggest that it might be time to retire. At its worst, the retirement-resistant faculty member enters a downward spiral. Sadly, I've watched it from up close. Their lack of productivity can result in stagnating compensation at just the moment when they need to be topping off a nest egg for retirement. In addition, decreasing effectiveness in the classroom can lead to worsening formal and informal evaluations from students, sometimes leading to declining course enrollments. I've seen colleagues stuck in this spiral and, wishing for them to end a long and illustrious career on a high note, I've hoped they'd make the decision to step down. Other faculty colleagues not in administrative positions, especially those with a close personal relationship to the senior colleague, may be able to offer such counsel. In your administrative role, however, you are not able to do so. I've had conversations with my dean about what kinds of incentives and compensation the institution might be willing to provide a senior colleague should they choose to retire, but that information had to remain in my back pocket while I waited for my colleague to approach me on the topic—a conversation that, unfortunately, we never had. Although biting your tongue may be difficult, it's easier than being hit with a lawsuit.

Providing Resources for Non-tenure-track Colleagues

Faculty colleagues who do not enjoy the supports and protection of the tenure track have needs that can be different from those of their tenure-track colleagues in significant ways. While this is true in the case of all your faculty colleagues, when mentoring and supporting your non-tenure-track faculty, you need to be aware that in some cases you're actually preparing them for their next job—ideally, one with the job security that your institution currently isn't offering them. At the same time, non-tenure-track appointments work well for some faculty members—those who wish to teach less than full time, for instance, and those at institutions with research demands who would prefer to focus on teaching alone. Especially under the pressures of declining tenure-track positions nationwide, most institutions are eager to voice their gratitude to and support for contingent faculty members. Too often, however, those sentiments aren't backed up with real resources. As department chair, of course, you're not in a position to force your institution to adopt more progressive policies regarding the working conditions of contingent faculty members (unless you can do so through your work in the institution's shared-governance structures), but there are things that you can do to make their work within the department as rewarding as possible.

My policy as chair in working with contingent faculty members has always been to act toward them not as an institutional mentor but more as a professional coach—a sort of extension of the role played most recently by their dissertation advisor. My job, as I see it—beyond ensuring that they meet the institution's expectations in terms of teaching and mentoring students—is to help them to continue to develop as professionals and try to find ways that their time at our institution, while teaching-intensive, can be productive in terms of their research and/or creative activity. In most departments, the hierarchy that rewards tenure-track faculty over contingent faculty means that support for professional development flows primarily, or entirely, to the tenure-track faculty, but you may have an opportunity to tip the balance to some degree by making conference and other research funding available to your contingent faculty. Some gestures require only a bit of ingenuity rather than financial resources. For example, although full-time contingent faculty typically teach a heavier load than their tenure-track peers, doubling up on their course preparations when possible can help them manage the workload. Two sections of the same course does not demand as much of an instructor as two different courses.*

Part of the loneliness of working off the tenure track is that you've been brought to the institution primarily for your capacity to teach and the institution generally pays very little attention to your research or creative work. Inviting a contingent faculty member to be a guest in one of your classes is one way to publicize their abilities as both a teacher and a scholar. But for an ambitious contingent faculty member, continued research or creative activity is de rigueur. In addition to supporting their scholarship materially, you can open up the intellectual resources of the department to your contingent faculty colleagues by inviting them to join a faculty reading group or give a scholarly talk to the department faculty. Doing their work with some sense of community and having opportunities for professional conversation will help break the isolation that is too often the contingent faculty member's lot. But it's probably important, too, to be clear about the limitations of the institution's commitment to its non-tenure-track faculty. I have worked with some contingent faculty over the years who seemed to believe that if they volunteered for multiple service assignments, they would endear themselves to the institution and

---

*Because I'm always anticipating that contingent faculty colleagues might be looking for a more permanent position, whether within the academy or outside it, I try to make the first move to offer a letter of recommendation (without suggesting that I'm showing them the door) and to schedule an opportunity to observe them teach if that isn't already on the calendar.

win some measure of job security. I can't recall a case in which that strategy was successful. Without devolving into paternalism, good mentoring probably requires that you share this hard truth with your colleague so that they can most effectively marshal their time and resources.

In the popular imagination, at least, a department chair is an authority figure who is responsible for completing bureaucratic paperwork, ensuring adherence to institutional policies, controlling resources, and setting department policy—making the department faculty eat their peas. But good department chairs establish and maintain clear lines of communication among all their faculty so that even the most junior and structurally marginalized have a voice and a role in shaping the department's agenda. The greatest reward in the work is certainly helping colleagues realize their potential and have the kinds of professional lives they envision for themselves. A good department chair, that is to say, spends a good bit more of their time mentoring than hectoring.

Chapter 3

Representing the Department to Students

The focus of this chapter is the work a chair does to foster vibrant relationships between the department and its students. At the smallest scale, of course, your department—which is to say, the teaching faculty in your department—enjoys a number of rich connections with your institution's students, whether they're majors in your department, students in your graduate program(s), or students from other majors who enroll in one or more of your department's offerings. These individual relationships are the foundation upon which anything larger must be built.

But that "larger" must, in fact, be built: it doesn't just happen. A department is more than just its faculty and the catalog listing of its course offerings and a major is more than a coherent path through those offerings. Rather, a department is, or endeavors to be, an intellectual and interpersonal experience that's greater than the sum of its parts. The well-being of your department—both as an administrative unit and as the faculty who teach together—depends on a thriving cohort of students to populate your courses and support other department events and initiatives. Ultimately, an academic department or program is a small ecosystem composed of a curriculum, a history, a budget, some shared space, and people (faculty, students, staff), and each must be attended to for the healthy functioning of the whole. And it's not enough to connect with each student in each seat in each of your department's courses individually. Students want to feel that they're part of something larger—that they're majors (for instance) in a department and that (to steal the old American Express slogan), membership has its privileges.

Part of your responsibility as chair of the department, then, is to foster that esprit de corps among your students. Students in your department's classes will have favorite instructors among your colleagues, but it's the department chair who represents the face of the department. Your colleagues may largely focus on their own courses and their own students, but as chair, all the lambs in the flock are your responsibility. Your colleagues will enjoy pedagogical relationships with the department's students, and although you will have those too, your work as chair needs to focus on the next level up, on students' experience in all the courses they take in your department. Ever since American higher education introduced the elective system in the early twentieth century, fragmentation of a student's education has been something of an occupational hazard. While it is difficult to ensure that a student's experiences in one classroom will be comparable to those in another department, division, or college, you're in a position as department chair to establish some coherence between the courses students take within your department. The most formal and durable way this is accomplished is the department's curriculum, including its requirements for the major (I'll address those in chapter 6). But much of the integrative work is in fact interpersonal work: extracurricular and co-curricular activities that create a sense of belonging and community among your students. That is my topic in this chapter.

The opportunities to build community for your students vary greatly with institutional type and size and available funding. Working to be inviting to students is one of the most important commitments a healthy and thriving department can make. This goes beyond being just available or accessible. I know that for some faculty this feels like pandering; I've heard that word used. Our job, these colleagues would suggest, is not to make our disciplines and departments attractive but only to ensure their integrity. In this way of thinking, anything that hints at marketing or branding—of currying favor with students, treating them like customers or consumers—smacks of academic bad faith.* I can appreciate that position in the abstract, but it belongs to a different era when higher education was reserved for the children of the upper and upper-middle classes who could afford four years of pure self-discovery without concern for their situation after graduation. To be sure, some students—and at some elite institutions, many students—still arrive with a commitment to what is often called learning for its own sake, and this type of disinterested intellectual pursuit combined with a broad, synthetic curriculum remains a kind of ideal at liberal arts colleges. But if we're committed to higher education playing a transformative role in our democratic society, faculty must also be willing—especially those of us who teach in "impractical" disciplines like the arts and humanities—to suggest some of the potential benefits of our curricula. Call it marketing if you like and lament it, but the more successful our institutions are in admitting a diverse body of students from nontraditional backgrounds, including low-income and first-generation students, the more it is incumbent upon us

*Speaking of branding and of commodifying your students (and faculty colleagues), the department I now teach in has long had a tradition of printing and distributing an annual departmental T-shirt. Each year a new design is selected in a contest among students. An enterprising student who identifies their major early can collect an ensemble of four; some faculty own more than a dozen.

to make the case for the difference that the knowledge our discipline provides can make in the real world.

Your Two Student Populations

As a metric of a department's health or relevance, the number of majors can be misleading. All faculty members, even those in disciplines with large numbers of majors, should advocate for more nuanced measures of a department's performance. Major enrollments can be fickle. Think back, for instance, to the huge bump in forensic science majors in the early 2000s in the wake of CBS's *CSI* franchise. And majors aren't the only students that most departments teach; some really essential departments teach more majors from other departments than their own students. (Increasingly, this is the fate of foreign language departments, for instance.) However, idealism notwithstanding, majors matter. They matter because they matter to your administration. They matter because they allow you and your colleagues to offer a curriculum that explores not just the surface but also the depth of your field and allow you to teach the material that got you excited about your discipline in the first place.

You'll need the support of your colleagues to recruit students to your major, but they should readily give it because the quality of their professional life depends on it. In all fields (even the most seemingly practical fields that are linked most closely to employment), students and their families will want assurance that rewarding jobs related to the major exist and the department should provide information about those career paths. Sometimes this can be done with the help of alums of your department, who may be willing to tell the story of their own route to their current work. Sometimes it's as simple as working with your career development office to provide up-to-date statistics on employment in the field, starting salaries, and so forth. Teaching, course offerings, and mentorship will attract students to your department who are interested in your field of study, but getting them to declare a major in your department requires you to help them imagine a future beyond the degree, when they can use what you're teaching them as the foundation for a rewarding career.

It's also important to attend to the needs of the other students in your care—students who may take one course or many courses in your department while satisfying the requirements for a major in another discipline. First, to reiterate, you should make the argument, often and forcefully, that your department's work with these students should be recognized through metrics other than number of majors (enrollments, for instance). But other data will help you meet the needs of these students as well as those of your majors—and most likely your admissions and career-development offices will have that data. For instance: Where do your students come to you from? What percentage of your students are first-generation or low-income students? What is your institution's year-over-year retention rate and four-, five-, and six-year graduation rate? Too often, we unconsciously assume that students who take and enjoy our classes, the ones who are interested in what we're interested in, are also like us in other ways, and some might be. But many are probably coming to the material from a very different background and point of view. Being aware of that context can help us make their connection to the material even more meaningful.

Student Liaisons

How can we invite students into our departments? When I came to my current institution as chair, many structures and traditions were in place that I was unfamiliar with. Some of them are quite brilliant. One of these is the position of student liaison within the department. When I started here, we chose two rising seniors in the major as student liaisons. A few years ago, we increased that group to four, adding two rising juniors. Now each liaison serves for two years, providing a bit more continuity in the role. In recent years, recognizing that faculty selection of the liaisons was liable to reproduce various kinds of bias, we have moved to an open call for applications and selection by faculty in consultation with current liaisons.

The student liaisons, as their title suggests, serve as intermediaries between the department faculty (especially the chair) and the department's students. The chair meets with them regularly to serve as an informal sounding board for requests, suggestions, complaints, and questions that bubble up from the student population. The chair can also run some departmental planning ideas past this "focus group" of students and get at least a preliminary sense of how various potential changes and faculty decisions might be received and get their (more or less) candid feedback on how the department is doing. The information flows in both directions. When I was chair, the liaisons' input often created extra work for me, but later I was glad I sought it out. Taking it seriously made the department better.

Especially over the past few years, it seems, our liaisons have been important in helping the faculty recognize events on the national and international stage that profoundly affect the lives of students and help us address them. Our student liaisons have spotlighted the outcome of state and national elections, the coordinated call to accountability of the #MeToo and Black Lives Matter movements, the shifting policies regarding undocumented immigrants and the trauma of studying as an undocumented student, and many other issues. We have then been able to partner with them to create programming and build policies that can help us alleviate harm.

One of the projects our student liaisons have historically helped us with is organizing and publicizing another long-standing department tradition, monthly late-afternoon events for our majors and other interested students. At the time I arrived, these were dubbed the monthly "English tea." We've since dropped that framing, since it suggests a very British, very white, Jane Austen-type cosplay. But we do still gather every month during the academic year, sometimes for a purely social gathering (coffee, lemonade, cookies) and sometimes with something more of a program in place. We schedule one gathering each semester in advance of the advising period, for instance, during which faculty members describe their next-term offerings for students and answer questions. In addition to these events created specifically for our students, we enjoy good student attendance at poetry and fiction readings and scholarly talks hosted by the department, Typically, the faculty member presiding at the event will make sure that some of the questions and comments during Q&A come from students. Depending on the size of your institution, there may also be opportunities to celebrate your senior majors in conjunction with commencement exercises. Here, the department hosts a reception the weekend of graduation that our graduates and their visiting family and friends are invited to. We host a similar reception each year for our alums in conjunction with our college's family weekend and alumni reunion weekend.

Student Participation in Department Life

Student involvement in faculty searches can also be a powerful means of demonstrating the department's strengths, commitments, and vision for the future to students. It also ensures that the candidates you're considering can connect with your students. Some institutions require student representatives on faculty search committees, some do not require it but allow it, and some, owing to issues around confidentiality, prohibit it. But if you're in a position to bring a student onto the search committee (whether in a voting or nonvoting role), it's worth all the complications it involves. I've found it especially valuable, when the circumstances make it possible, to appoint a student who has made clear their intention to pursue a scholarly career (or in departments with graduate programs, an advanced PhD student in the field that's being searched). For better or worse, they'll come to understand the intricacies of the search process quite intimately.

And whether or not students participate on the search committee itself, they should certainly be encouraged to help the department assess its candidates in public lectures, teaching demonstrations, and other public fora during a campus interview. While faculty members are well situated by virtue of their own teaching experience to judge a candidate's teaching ability and potential, there's one thing your students are certainly better able to gauge than faculty are, and that's a candidate's comfort in talking with students when there are no other faculty in the room. When candidates are not performing a teacherly role for the department faculty, are they able to connect in a comfortable way with your students? Are they interested in your students? In my department, our on-campus interviews always include a late-morning teaching demonstration that's followed by an informal lunch in the dining halls with interested students. A student member of the search committee serves as host of that lunch and then meets with the department chair afterward to share impressions of the candidate (which are also solicited independently from students via an anonymous online survey).

When I was chair of our department, students would frequently approach me with their own ideas for events, sometimes through their liaisons and sometimes independently. To the extent possible, it felt important to say yes to let the students know that they had agency in the department. We would provide modest funds, for instance, for refreshments at a reading group, and we might provide a faculty speaker for a student gathering. If your building has the capacity, you can dedicate a room as a study space for students. My department is fortunate to be housed in a gracious old building that has its own small library. Students love to congregate there, but traditionally it was only open from 8:00 a.m. to 5:00 p.m. Monday through Friday, and that, of course, is not when students wanted to be there. At their suggestion, we were able to get facilities to fit the door with a card reader that allows 24/7 access to the room and spent some department funds on some soft furniture and a networked printer. The library has become a pretty lively gathering spot for students in and around our discipline. It's not without cost; there's sometimes a bit of tidying up to do on a Monday morning, for instance. And one time we discovered that the centralized HVAC system was shutting down at night and students were opening the windows—and as a result, squirrels were taking shelter among the furniture. But hosting this space encourages our students to think of the department as a home base, and that has an intangible value all its own.

Student Advising

Especially in large universities, student advising is often handled by professional staff who focus on that activity alone. At smaller institutions, advising is handled at the department level, and in many departments, especially those with a single faculty administrator, the chair coordinates the department's student advising. Beyond any advising of individual students that you may do, you'll also be looked to as the person with the best working knowledge of the department's curriculum and major requirements. You'll also probably be in the position to make decisions about nonstandard curricula your students may request. In the departments I've served in, the chair has the authority to authorize credit toward the major for transfer and study-abroad courses, for instance, and to approve substitutions in the major requirements.* Even a faculty colleague who has taught in the department for decades might not have kept up with the latest changes to major requirements and college-wide curricula and therefore may not be in a position to give their advisees definitive answers

---

*At one of the state institutions where I taught, articulation agreements were in place with other parts of the state's higher education system so that (for instance) courses taken at Western State were immediately "translated" for a student transferring to Northern State. Even in the case of such agreements, though, students transferring from outside the state system will present credentials that an experienced faculty member will need to examine and interpret.

to their questions. For these reasons and more, your attention will be required during student advising periods and intermittently throughout the academic year even if you're not currently carrying an advisee load.

Depending on your institution's culture and reward system, some faculty colleagues may cut corners on their student advising; I've seen that happen. In a previous job, back in the days before computerized registration, we were required to meet with students to discuss their plans for the next semester and sign a course request form that was submitted to the registrar after we had that conversation. Two doors down from my office, a colleague would hang a box from his doorhandle during pre-registration advising; he simply told his advisees to drop off their cards for his signature. To be sure, advising can be something of a nuisance, especially with undergraduates, some of whom seem congenitally incapable of remembering an appointment they've scheduled. But the advising your majors receive from your colleagues is a crucial component of your department's esprit de corps.

The relative confidentiality of the advising meeting can also create a temptation for faculty members to be indiscrete about the perceived failings of their colleagues. Students will naturally enough ask for recommendations about which courses and faculty to take, especially those who are not in the major or have not been at the institution very long, and they may give vent to their dissatisfaction with various of your colleagues. I've not always gotten along with all of my colleagues and I've worked with some who I thought were not effective and/or dedicated teachers. However, I've kept a strict policy of never discouraging a student from enrolling in a particular colleague's course. Especially in contentious departments, this strikes me as the minimum bar for collegiality and fairness to our students. As department chair, you must be diligent about following up with any colleagues who are not honoring it.

Handling Grievances

This leads naturally enough into discussing an even more uncomfortable role department chairs are occasionally called upon to play: serving formally as the referee when students voice dissatisfaction with their faculty members (and informally when faculty grouse about students). The chair also plays a role when a colleague raises concerns about a student's academic honesty (e.g., plagiarism). These are topics it is difficult to generalize about across institutions; you will need to be guided by the policies of your college or university. The stakes of a misstep can be quite high. As soon as possible, familiarize yourself with the various student and faculty grievance procedures in place at your institution, including Title IX complaints (which are handled outside the department), and your role and responsibilities within those processes.

All faculty members who assume positions of academic leadership—provosts and deans most especially, but department chairs too—report that one of the most dispiriting aspects of the new role is learning things about colleagues they never wanted to know. For a chair, this often comes about because students will bring complaints to you about your colleagues' teaching, mentoring, or professionalism. To be sure, all faculty have had some experience of this—you walk into your classroom a few minutes early and overhear students complaining about a colleague's teaching or, just as likely, praising a colleague's teaching. In that situation, your role as a faculty member is probably just to pretend that you're not hearing anything (unless it's praise). When you are a chair, however, that's not an option when a student makes an appointment to speak with you about problems they're having with one of your colleagues.

Your first move in such a meeting, of course—after hearing the student's grievance and ensuring that you've heard them correctly—is to acknowledge the student's feelings without taking sides and recognize that it may have been difficult for them to come to you. Next, ask what steps they've taken to bring these concerns to their instructor's attention. The power imbalance between student and faculty member can make the idea of initiating such a conversation quite daunting; indeed, the student has no doubt had to overcome some reservations even to bring their concerns to you. For a student, bringing their concerns to their classroom instructor adds an extra dimension of anxiety to the conversation, since the student and the instructor are forced to interact with one another on a regular basis and the instructor is in a position to grade the student's work and award or withhold credit. All of these forces can make it difficult for students to approach their instructors with their complaints, but I make it a policy never to speak about these concerns with a student who hasn't brought them first to their instructor. (The one exception is a complaint of sexual harassment.)

There are at least two reasons for this. First, of course, you're hoping that when a student brings their concerns to their instructor, they will get satisfaction, that a misunderstanding will be cleared up or the instructor will make a small tweak to their classroom practice or the classroom environment and you'll be off the hook for arbitrating the dispute. But even if this isn't the result, it will help you avoid pursuing parallel but never converging conversations with the student and your colleague. And just as I will not hear a grievance from a student who hasn't attempted to reach out to the instructor in question, so I won't—and you should never—lean into a student's recitation of the facts of the case before you've had a chance to speak with the instructor.

So you're sitting with a student who has brought a complaint about their instructor, or at least their instruction. You'll need to listen actively and carefully. Take notes and ask follow-up and clarifying questions, but do not take a side, no matter how cut and dried the issue might initially seem. You should make it a rule for yourself that in an initial conversation, you will do nothing but gather information. Make sure you understand the precise nature of the complaint and capture the details of any evidence the aggrieved party may present, then thank them for seeking you out, promise to conduct your own investigation to corroborate the details, explain the process, and let them know when they can expect to hear something further from you. And one further thing, something I've often forgotten: ask the student what outcome they're looking for. Sometimes the ask is out of proportion to the perceived offense ("no, we won't fire Prof. Mendoza because their slides can't be read from the back of the room"), but often you'll find out that all they want is someone to listen to their experiences.

But in this forum, provide no expression of sympathy, no betrayal of skepticism, no avowal of righteous indignation. Take them seriously and make sure they understand the institutional process. Think of Sgt. Joe Friday from the TV series *Dragnet*: you're there for "just the facts" (or your informant's version of them). For some of us, this is incredibly difficult. I've sat through such conversations feeling deeply skeptical owing to my knowledge of the student or the instructor or to the implausible nature of the story being unfolded. I've also sat through these conversations with a deep sense of déjà vu because I've heard similar complaints about the instructor from other students. If a student who I know to be hardworking, open-hearted, and honest comes to me despite some obvious trepidation to complain about their treatment by a faculty colleague who I think is an ogre, every fiber of my being wants to comfort them or even contribute a damning anecdote of my own about Prof. Jackass. But I can't.

Once the student has presented their information, thank them for coming forward, promise to investigate the charges, and let them know what the next steps look like. Then you'll need to talk to the faculty member in question without identifying the source of the complaint. In a small department or a small course, your faculty colleague may guess correctly who has lodged the complaint; all you can do in that case is refuse to corroborate their identity. Often, thankfully, the bare fact that the department chair has asked for a conversation and conveyed the bad news of a student complaint is all that's necessary to get the faculty member's attention and for the situation to be addressed. Sometimes you will discover that a student has misconstrued a faculty member's words or actions and a simple clarification from the faculty member is all that's required. Sometimes a faculty member will instead double down on a policy or a behavior that you think is ill advised. Because we enjoy the protections of academic freedom, the most you can do is bring the complaint to the faculty member. You're not in a position to stipulate changes in classroom demeanor or grading practices, for instance, unless they're clearly in violation of your institution's stated policies.

If the instructor confirms the student's charge—that student work isn't being returned in a timely way, for instance—the fact that the issue has been aired in front of a colleague (and in this case, the chair) may be enough to get the desired result. In that situation, I would report back to the student that I'd discussed the issue with their instructor and ask the student to be in touch again if the problem persisted. You'll have to use your judgment, of course, about deciding not to meet with an instructor over a complaint that even if true isn't grievable: the fact that a student finds Byzantine art history boring or that the exams in molecular biology are "too hard" (assuming that a reasonable percentage of their classmates are passing those same exams) doesn't warrant follow-up.

However, if the instructor denies the validity of the student's charge—the most common student complaint I've heard over the years has to do with the perception of unfair grading—you're now really in the position of arbitrator. It's difficult to generalize about what this next step might look like, given the wide range of things a student might be concerned about. Different scenarios suggest different kinds of fact-finding and remedy. In the case of a grade dispute, you might (with the instructor's permission, out of consideration for academic freedom) offer to review the work yourself or ask a department colleague to do so. The trick in this instance and in all instances of student complaints is to strike a balance and be seen as an honest broker. In that role, your responsibility would be to listen supportively to the student's experience and to take seriously the possibility of a colleague's need for constructive feedback without encroaching on that colleague's prerogative to deliver course material and assess student learning in the manner they judge most appropriate as long as they continue to meet their responsibilities to their students. In most institutional settings, a student can seek relief at another administrative level if they don't find satisfaction in the departmental process, but for all kinds of reasons, you and your colleagues are best served by resolving things within the department if at all possible.

And then you'll need to report back to the student, whether in person or via email. When you've done all that you can—secured a correction or clarification or apology from the faculty member or simply made them aware of the complaint without any response on their part—you should tell the student of the outcome and inform them about what avenues of appeal remain open to them if they're not satisfied (for example, taking their complaint to the dean of students office or an ombudsperson).

All this presupposes an individual student coming to you with a grievance, but often department faculty and the chair are made aware of complaints through their liaisons or by a group of aggrieved students setting up a meeting or even contact by a concerned parent. When dealing with students, the advice would be the same: gather information, betray no opinion, follow up, report back. Parents are a different, and difficult, matter. My firm policy is that complaints about teaching have to come from students, and although I'm willing to listen to a parent discuss the challenges their student is facing, the parent doesn't have standing—only their student does. If after talking with me a parent is able to encourage their student to meet with me, then we can start a process; otherwise, we cannot.

Student-Faculty Retreats

Wise department chairs long ago recognized the value of occasionally getting their faculty colleagues away from campus for big-picture conversations. Sometimes a setting that is too familiar can reinforce familiar lines of thinking. (I address this subject in chapter 7.) For the same reason, it's a great treat, when possible, to gather with your department's students in an informal setting, one that is ideally off campus. My current institution is fortunate to have a couple of properties that have been donated over the years by alumni of the college. One of them is a rustic cabin located in a nearby recreation area that is a perfect place for a weekend retreat that's available by reservation for departments and student groups. Many departments have a tradition of taking their majors there for a time of group bonding and relationship building—an opportunity for students to get to know one another and their faculty outside the campus setting and for faculty to get a peek into what their students' unstructured time looks like. When my department goes, we cook together, hike, play board games, play music, read, and, of course, look at our phones, despite the terrible cell signal. If nothing else, these retreats remind students of the full humanity of their faculty members—and faculty members the same about their students. The twin projects of diversifying the student body and the faculty run on different time scales, which can create an atmosphere of mutual distrust. After a successful retreat, however, everyone returns to the classroom with a fuller understanding of each other. (Although I'm not entirely sure how it helps my students to know that I snore.)

Working with Prospective Students

Current students aren't the only students we should be thinking about. Although it becomes impractical at very large institutions, some small schools and departments may have the opportunity to work with their admissions staff to reach out to admitted students who have indicated an interest in their department. In the past, I have volunteered to make phone calls to prospective students considering an English major; sometimes I have emailed each of these students instead. Often, having the opportunity to connect with a member of the faculty is meaningful for these students, and we're in a better position to answer questions about our departments and programs than admissions staff are. There's a good chance that these admitted students will matriculate at your institution, if not necessarily in your department. Besides providing something of an entrée for the student in the new school year, I appreciated having an initial conversation under my belt when I met the student on campus for the first time.

That's the narrow end of the prospective-student funnel. At the other end, and seemingly more each year, are the students who visit your campus with family members (typically during the spring or summer of their junior year in high school) and either ask for a meeting or simply show up at your office. Faculty rarely welcome these interruptions, and I learned over time to put in some safeguards—either to announce at the start that I had another engagement in 20 minutes or email our department coordinator at the start of the meeting and ask them to call me in half an hour so that I had a pretext for breaking it off. These campus visits, which our former director of admissions referred to as the new great American family vacation, certainly help students and their families feel more confident about one of the most important decisions of the student's young life. But I'm skeptical about the return on investment on the faculty member's time. Students and families that make the trip to your campus deserve some of your—or at least someone's—time and attention, just not too much. (I once had a student and her parents in my office for two hours during the summer. And she never enrolled here.)

Staying Connected to Alums

The final category of students you should be cultivating relationships with are former students. As I write these words, a former student has just published his first novel and my department colleagues and I are bursting with pride. Because I've kept in touch with Tom—I was the advisor for his senior thesis and chair of the department during his time here—I sent out a quick congratulatory note. Beyond that, we arranged for him to return to campus to give a reading and meet with current students. For the most part, alums love an invitation to return to their alma mater (and will often cover the cost of their own travel), and current students appreciate having examples of how their classroom experiences can translate into success in the real world, especially from alums of relatively recent vintage.

There are a number of good reasons to stay in contact with your department's students as they move out into the world. They can be powerful examples of and spokespeople for the transformational power of your department's mentorship. They also help you spotlight for colleagues across the institution, especially campus administrators, the good teaching your department is doing. Outside review teams, too, will typically inquire about the career paths of your grads, as will regional accreditors. And as colleges and universities have long known, alumni are an institution's most reliable source of long-term giving, especially those who have enjoyed career success after graduation and attribute at least a portion of that success to what they learned in their time with you.

Because these relationships can be not just affective but in fact financial, most institutions guard their alumni jealously—often, even from the departments they studied in. An advancement office that has been carefully cultivating a potential alumni donor doesn't want a financially naïve faculty member inadvertently complicating an ongoing conversation and undermining many months, sometimes even years, of hard work. (As Al Pacino said in *Glen-*

garry Glen Ross, "You never open your mouth till you know what the shot is.") This reasonable concern on the part of your development/advancement team has two very practical implications:

1. Whether or not your advancement office is willing to share alumni data with you, your department must collect and maintain its own data. Many colleges and universities now allow students to keep their institutional (.edu) email addresses after they graduate precisely because it aids in the project of locating alums. Apart from bare contact data, you'll want to keep track of your alumni's career arcs if possible. This is made easier if you create a LinkedIn group for your department and its alums.

2. Even though you'll be able to contact your alums if you've followed the advice in point 1, *keep your advancement staff and/or alumni affairs office in the loop when you do so.* You should never contact an alumnus with a direct financial request without routing it through your advancement office. One of the cardinal principles of institutional fund-raising is that there be a single point of contact that approves and coordinates the "asks." And even when your contact is not of a financial nature—my reaching out to Tom, for instance, to congratulate him on the publication of his novel and inviting him to come back to campus—your contact in the advancement office should be kept apprised of these communications. They sometimes contain information that is valuable to that office in their ongoing development efforts and enable them to keep up-to-date records on alums.

It is a truth universally acknowledged—to pick up again, for a minute, the Jane Austen vibe—that our students are the reason for our existence. We know it in our hearts, and when we are reminded of it we immediately affirm its truth. But given the many other things that hail our attention, we can become distracted. As department chair, you hope to have an important role in advancing the careers of your faculty colleagues and in advocating for your department's needs in administrative conversations about various kinds of resources. But a department doesn't consist primarily of a collection of professors: those professors are there to foster the learning of the real department, the students that enroll in its courses.

Chapter 4

Working with Staff and Other Departmental Administrators

Department chairs occupy a unique position within their departments and their institutions—and as an English professor and all-around linguistic fussbudget, I use the term "unique" advisedly. When my provost at a former institution was commiserating with me during a rough patch, she told me she believed that department chair was the most difficult role in the academy. At the time I chalked her comment up to compassion; now I know it's true. Department chairs have only a few scattered peers across campus who usually work in almost complete isolation from each other. They do their work at a vertiginous node in the web of relationships on campus: they report up (to directors, deans, and/or provosts), across (to faculty colleagues), and down—to students, in one manner of speaking, and to staff, in another.

Let me hasten to add that if you object to the idea that department chairs "talk down" to their staff (never mind their students), you absolutely should. By "talking down" here I'm not referring to condescension; I am acknowledging the reality of the institution's hierarchies of power, which find staff far less privileged than the faculty they work with (and sometimes the students they support) in terms of salary, working conditions, job security, prestige— pretty much everything. A chair's relationships with faculty colleagues, though sometimes fraught, are at least nominally peer relationships: relationships with staff are explicitly not. And this presents a department chair with some significant challenges.

Two Categories of Direct Reports

Depending upon the size and mission of your department, you may be in the position of supervising two different kinds of department staff. They go by different names at different institutions, but broadly, the two different arms I'll be talking about here are faculty members with formal department-level administrative assignments and staff members who are not faculty.

In a small department, the chair is often the only faculty administrative position. But when the size of the department (in terms of student majors and minors, enrollments, programs and programming, and faculty) gets beyond a certain point or its mission becomes sufficiently complex, some faculty administrative positions are typically created to help manage the workload of the department. These faculty administrators report directly to the chair. Sometimes these positions are responsible for a portion of the curriculum or student population (for example, a director of undergraduate studies or a director of graduate studies) and sometimes these are directors of distinctive programs, tracks, or curricula within the department. Sometimes departments with distinctive missions have a need for their own distinctive faculty administrators. A department that manages a large internship program, for instance, may need a director to oversee that part of the program; graduate programs, especially those that confer the PhD, may require the services of a faculty job-placement coordinator. And very large departments, regardless of their mission or focus, may designate a vice chair or associate chair with a portfolio that varies from unit to unit. Typically, faculty administrative positions within the department carry some sort of incentive for the faculty occupant: a reduced teaching load, professional development funds, an annual stipend, accelerated leave accrual, or some combination of these.

Ordinarily, these faculty administrators are selected and appointed by the chair, who issues a call for nominations and self-nominations to all eligible members of the department faculty. Often a newly elected chair will use the period between their selection and the start of their term to put together their administrative team. It's generally understood that current department administrators will be willing to step down from their positions when a new chair begins their term, although of course you're welcome to ask them to stay on if they're doing good work, they enjoy the role, and you work well with them. In some cases, a faculty member's willingness to serve as chair will depend on an advance agreement with colleagues that they will be willing to serve in key department leadership roles, so that a chair is elected or appointed almost as the top of a "ticket."

Having other faculty administrators working alongside you means that you'll also have to supervise the work they do with you to some degree and provide regular feedback. Many institutions don't have a formal evaluation for these department administrators in place apart from the annual evaluation that's common to all faculty. Instead, you'll want to give regular, informal feedback to those leading the department with you so that you're getting what you need from them and they're working with a clear sense of what you're looking for from them. In the one department I chaired that was large enough for such a structure, I met every Monday morning, even if only briefly sometimes, with our department administrators to discuss concerns, deadlines, upcoming events, progress on various projects, and so forth. I supplemented these regular, formal meetings as needed with informal conversations in the various administrators' offices. If I had a question about enrollment trends in the major, for instance,

I might just wander down to the office of the director of undergraduate studies to hear their thoughts and ask them to pull together some data if the situation warranted it.

Few of us who find ourselves chairing departments have had any formal training in supervising others, faculty or staff, apart from mandatory annual sexual harassment training. Working with faculty introduces the added dynamic that if they're tenured (and at an institution that awards tenure, strong preference should be given to appointing department administrators who already hold tenure, lest the progress of a junior faculty member be hampered), there's little in terms of hard power to be done with a director who isn't performing. For that reason, it's important to make the most of the soft power at your disposal—cultivate a close and collegial working relationship, check in often, and be generous with your praise and chary with your criticisms.

Working with Departmental Staff

The possible range of departmental responsibilities for staff is broader than it is for faculty in administrative roles. One or more of the department's faculty administrators, including the chair, may have an administrative assistant, for example. Depending on the size and complexity of the unit, the department might support an office manager, a personnel manager, a finance/grants administrator, a purchasing specialist, a laboratories director, or a scheduler. The more specialized the department, the more individualized these roles can become. Some very large professional and pre-professional departments even employ their own fundraiser.* My Monday morning meetings with faculty administrators were regularly followed by a meeting with staff and with much the same agenda. In part, this gave the staff a natural opportunity to remind me of impending deadlines and information

---

*Both the job descriptions and the titles of these various roles vary widely in different institutional contexts. The names used here are generic.

or approvals or paperwork they needed from me in order to keep their projects moving forward.

Hiring staff poses a different set of challenges from those involved in appointing faculty administrators within the department. Unless you (or they) are quite new to the department, you'll know any faculty candidates pretty well, but candidates for staff positions typically come from outside the department or off campus and are largely unknowns. Some institutions are very good at advertising staff positions widely, so that there's a rich pool of applicants from which to choose—some with campus experience, some without. At other institutions, the applications sent over from HR can be almost entirely from on-campus candidates looking to move up or move out of an undesirable position. Letters of recommendation can help to a degree as you try to discriminate between ambitious staff moving up the ranks and those who have bounced around unhappily among different units. A careful reading of the résumé will also give you some hints. But be alert: having a staff member leave for another department is always easier than firing an underperforming employee, and a current supervisor's letter of recommendation may be blandly covering over inadequacies in order to move someone out of the unit.

When setting up interviews for staff positions, think about the new staff member's responsibilities and colleagues. Is the position student-facing? Invite a student to sit in on the interviews and provide feedback, ask questions that assess their experience in working with students, and provide some scenarios that ask them to think about how best to help students achieve their goals. If the new staff member will work directly with you or with another faculty administrator, and/or with other professional staff members, consider having one or more of them involved in the interviews. Unless you're hiring someone into a new position, you will already have experience working with someone in the position and know what they did well and did poorly and what you'd like to find in a new colleague. Case studies and scenarios based on real experience can be invaluable here. If you're hoping to find a problem-solver to work with you, give them some problems to solve in their interview.

Unlike the faculty administrators in the department, your staff colleagues will be subject to annual performance reviews of some kind and it will be your task to prepare these. Perhaps the institutions I've worked in are not representative, but my experience is that staff evaluations feel very high stakes for the staff members but seem to go all but unread by the administrators who order them up. My very first experience of being evaluated myself in the academy has profoundly shaped the way I've approached all the evaluations I've subsequently had to provide. It took place during my first term teaching a stand-alone course as a graduate student, and a faculty member who would later serve on my dissertation committee came to observe a class session.* Although it's been many years now, my recollection is that the class went reasonably well, but what I still remember vividly is how my mentor handled the evaluation. They had of course taken notes on the class. They invited me to their office for a debriefing and they said, in effect, "There are things that will go into the observation that I write up and put in the department files—and there are things that I'd like to tell you, that are just for you." Essentially, almost all of the constructive criticism that they had for me was delivered orally and never found its way into the written record, which detailed the things that I was doing well in my teaching. There were, in essence, two evaluations: one for me and one for the administration.

That's for the most part how I think about staff evaluations today, at least for staff members who are doing a good or great job in their work with me. Since there are few rewards attached to these evaluations and a lot of anxiety, it doesn't seem to me fair to

---

*I'm just realizing that in my seven years of graduate training, my dissertation adviser never saw me teach. That says something about the priorities of graduate training.

use them to rehearse minor grievances. Instead, I like to play the long game and build the case for raises and promotions when they're warranted. If I have significant concerns about a staff member's performance and the first time they're hearing about them from me is the annual performance review, then I'm not doing my job. (Similarly, if I'm delighted with their work and the annual review is the first time they're hearing of it, I'm remiss in an equal and opposite direction.) In a department meeting or via an email solicitation, I always invite department faculty to share any feedback they wish about the performance of the staff—I'm not, after all, the only one who works with them. If they are to do this in an informed way, it's important that you share with them the staff member's self-assessment, the first step in the evaluation process, so they have a better understanding of how the staff member's work may have changed since they were last reviewed.

The HR department may tell you to use the top of the scale only sparingly in evaluations. In my experience, the folks in academic affairs are much less concerned about student grade inflation than HR is about staff "grade inflation." Be that as it may, use the annual review as a place to document the accomplishments and strengths of staff members who are meeting or exceeding expectations and to lay out goals for the year ahead.

On the other hand, in the unfortunate situation where a staff colleague is not making the grade, the annual review becomes something quite different. A paper trail (even if it's in fact electronic) that documents shortcomings in a staff member's performance may be the only way you can ultimately terminate such an employee if their performance doesn't improve. A critical evaluation is difficult for most of us to deliver and even more difficult in person than in writing, but common courtesy and collegiality requires the former and the bureaucracy requires the latter. If you're identifying shortcomings in a staff colleague's performance, it's important to also provide possible remedies, such as staff trainings, professional development opportunities, or working with a coach or mentor.

Who evaluates the chair in their role as supervisor of staff? Ideally, it's those you supervise, although the power differential can make candid observations difficult for staff members. Some staff evaluation forms provide space for staff members to respond to supervisors' criticism and suggest ways that supervisors can help implement the changes the evaluation is asking for. Some of this feels like a matter of the tone you have established with those you are supervising. There's no use, of course, in ruling like a martinet 364 days a year and then suddenly asking for candid feedback. ("I'm all ears. Seriously.") Your larger patterns of behavior and treating your staff with respect will tacitly invite them to help you do your job better in all the ways they can, even when that means offering some constructive feedback. If they don't feel free to offer it on their own, no invitation from you is going to bring it out.

Finally, in addition to advice from your staff, your institution will make opportunities to sharpen your skills available to you. At my institution at least, I get several emails every month inviting me to attend training for supervisors. Attend these trainings even when it's optional. Read campus climate surveys and think about how the picture they paint affects (and reflects) your staff. Take the job of supervising your staff as seriously as you ask them to take the job of supporting you.

The Delicate Art of Delegation

For most faculty members, becoming a "boss" is a weird and unsettling experience. We're not used to having supervisory authority over anyone, and most of us have no real experience in delegating work to others. This is perhaps somewhat different in the lab science disciplines (for instance), where research tends to be more collaborative, carried out in research groups, or shared with graduate students. But in the humanities, we tend to pursue our work in relative isolation. Even using graduate assistants for any but the most clerical of tasks is uncommon. Suddenly, when we take on the role of chair, we have someone (or part of someone) whose job it is to assist us in doing ours. At first, it feels like a luxury—and it is. But if not approached thoughtfully, it can quickly become a liability rather than an asset.

I probably should confess, for the sake of transparency, that until quite recently I made very poor use of the staff members I supervised. Visible, public planning isn't really my long suit; decades of organization seminars and software have left little imprint on me. For that reason, I've long felt it difficult to share my workload with someone else, not because I'm greedy (although perhaps I am) and not because I'm a control freak (this I certainly am), but because the work in front of me tends to remain ill defined until it's really too late to invite anyone else into it. Hence, one of the secrets of working effectively with staff and faculty administrative colleagues is that you need to be more thoughtful about the work to be accomplished and work with a longer horizon than when you're slogging away on your own.

I'm fortunate now to work with an associate director in a relationship that feels more like a collaboration, an intellectual partnership, than a faculty-staff relationship (although they are a staff member). When I think about what's made the difference, I must admit that a large part of it is owing to them. They know that I'm inclined to keep tasks hidden in my head instead of in our shared planner, and they've become adept at coaxing that to-do list out of me at regular intervals so that they can figure out what role they might play. And they take a personal and professional interest in the work we're trying to do and have thrown themself into it without reservation. Of course, working with a staff member who makes the unit's mission their own is an incredible gift. But passion for the work can't be made a job criterion. It's nice if you get it, but if you don't (and many of us won't), we still need to get the department's business done.

Some Dos and Don'ts

Here are a few suggestions for working well with the staff member(s) supporting you as chair that have grown largely out of disappointing experiences.

One. Give your staff colleagues assignments of increasing complexity and give them incrementally more autonomy in carrying out those assignments so you can discover what work they do best and enjoy most. I've worked with staff colleagues who were absolute wizards with a spreadsheet; I've also worked with some who were completely unfazed when their formulas returned preposterous results. ("Wait. We're $170K in the red?") In the course of my administrative work, I've learned to put together a pretty sophisticated Excel sheet. If I'm working with an assistant whose skills in a particular area I question—if, for instance, delegating a budget project to them means that I'll be worrying about the work they'll produce—I keep that assignment for myself and hand something to them that's more squarely in their wheelhouse. Delegating isn't just a synonym for offloading the work you don't want to do yourself; it's a rather more sophisticated process of realizing that you have a body of work to accomplish and two bodies/two minds with two overlapping but distinct skill sets to bring to that work. Wise delegation lies in figuring out how to maximize the productivity of the pseudo-couple that you create when working with a partner, not in exploiting your greater authority by pushing "downhill" all the tasks that strike you as too menial. Although it's a standard that's difficult to live up to, I try never to delegate to a staff colleague a task that I wouldn't myself be willing to do. That's just how my mother raised me.

Two. But there are limits to this sort of win-win delegation. In the current environment, you would never hire an administrative staff colleague who wasn't fluent in basic computer skills, who couldn't read and work with an Excel spreadsheet, even if they're not expert in assembling a complex one. And if part of their job description is to help manage correspondence, they'd better be able to produce an appropriate and gracious email.* In a collaboration between two capable people, there should be some room for give and take regarding who is responsible for what, although some matters (faculty hiring and evaluation, for instance) cannot be delegated to staff. But sharing such responsibility does require two capable people.

Three. Because we enjoy a great deal of autonomy in our faculty roles—indeed, the ability to work under our own direction and supervision is at least one of the enticements that drew most of us to this work—it can feel difficult to supervise staff colleagues whose work and work time is much more structured and surveilled than ours. Most faculty members are exempt employees: we're salaried and are expected to work a full work week (however we or our institution understand what that means) without punching a time clock; we don't get paid overtime. Most staff positions, in contrast, are non-exempt (shorthand for "not exempt from overtime compensation"); staff employees have to record their work hours and have those hours vetted and approved by a supervisor, and that's you. Of course it feels uncomfortable.

But if you think about it a little more carefully, we faculty don't really work fully autonomously, either. And I'm not referring just to the quiet monitoring that goes on continually during the pretenure period of a tenure-track faculty member's career or the surveillance between tenure and promotion—times when, while we're certainly working under observation and feel the weight of the hierarchy, we're not exactly directly reporting to a supervisor. Just today, for instance, I got the page proofs for an article I've written for an edited collection. I have to review the proofs, mark any corrections or changes, and get them back to the

---

*Because I'm a writer, this is the job I find hardest to delegate: I want the written communication coming out of my office to reflect my own values and personality as a writer, and no one else sounds quite like me (and most likely, they would not want to). I insist on doing almost all my own writing.

editor, and I have a hard deadline. And the volume editor, in turn, must submit the full manuscript back to the publisher, where they too have an editor. Much faculty work takes place without any obvious deadlines or reporting structures, but we do contend with those, too. It's not just our staff who are held accountable by supervisors—to some degree, we all are.

Four. While few faculty members chair their department for more than five or six years, some staff coordinators in the department have been at the helm for 30 years or more. On the day that you assume your role, you immediately have more power and authority than the most senior staff member in your department, but they likely know much more about many aspects of department administration than you do or ever will. Be teachable: honor and solicit their experience. It will save you a lot of heartache. Although it's true that some staff members who have been in their roles for a long time will become inflexible and stuck in routine ways of doing their work (as will some faculty members), sometimes when the staff member who has handled the financials in your department for decades tells you that a certain expense won't be approved, they know what they're talking about. Sometimes this is called institutional memory, which to me always carried a whiff of ageism. Call it what you want, but you'll hit the ground running much quicker and you'll do your job much better and with less unnecessary friction if you carefully listen to it when it's offered and seek it out when it's not.

Five. It's your job to protect your staff members from unfair demands from or unfair treatment by your faculty colleagues. In over three decades working in higher education, I've been disheartened time and again to see the way my faculty colleagues, many of whom pride themselves on their solidarity with the working class (for instance), treat staff members like dirt. If a faculty colleague is making things unpleasant for your staff, you need to intervene to protect them. You have authority and job security that make it possible for you to stick your neck out in ways your staff colleagues just can't. Of course, if faculty colleagues have justifiable complaints about the performance of staff members, that's your concern too; you're not there simply to protect and defend the staff. But in my experience, the power imbalance makes the treatment of staff more urgent for you to attend to.

Six. It's not possible for you to extend to your staff colleagues all the benefits you enjoy as a faculty member. Faculty members work under conditions that are unimaginable to the vast majority of the workforce. But there are ways for you to share at least some of the privilege that you enjoy with those who support you in your work. Be creative. For better or worse, you are the eyes and ears that your institution keeps on your staff colleagues. If you can arrange something that works for you and your staff, that's the end of the discussion. So you might be flexible about work hours when the need arises or allow occasional days of working from home.* Faculty members at most institutions can take a "vacation day" any day they're not teaching and don't have a scheduled meeting—it's so loose we don't even accrue vacation days because we don't need them. Staff, on the other hand, need your permission to take even the vacation days they've accrued. Give it, even if it creates something of a hardship for you. If there's any way for you to say yes, say it. Do your best with the authority that you've been given to soften some of the jarring discrepancies that the institution has created between your working conditions and those of the staff you work with.

---

*As this book goes into production in the last weeks of 2021, we're still in the grip of a worldwide pandemic that, no matter when (or whether) it recedes, has left its mark on business as usual at colleges and universities, along with the rest of our institutions. We now know, for instance, that we needn't all be in the same room to have a productive meeting and that our desk jobs can, to an extent, be conducted from a variety of different desks. I have chosen not to write separately about chairing under the cloud of COVID-19, but if nothing else, it has taught us important lessons that we can carry forward into our post-pandemic reality about the very different situations we're all negotiating outside work and about the importance of flexibility in meeting our students and doing our work.

Seven. Staff are (in my experience) paid pretty poorly, and this is compounded if their supervisor doesn't thoughtfully assess their work in annual performance evaluations and regularly support raises and/or promotions when they're warranted. Also, provide professional development opportunities for your staff members when possible or appropriate.

Eight. National Administrative Professionals Day is the Wednesday of the last full week of April. It's perhaps the one date or deadline that should be on your calendar that no sensitive chair can expect their administrative assistant to remind them of. Get it on your calendar yourself and recognize the work of the staff that you work with in some way that will be meaningful to them. Any gift or recognition you give will come out of your own pocket, but if you itemize your taxes, the expense is deductible. If they are underpaid, it's the institution that's undervaluing them. Make sure you show them on your own how much you value their contribution to the department and to your own success as chair.*

Nine. Local cultures vary, but it's always been important to me that the staff I supervised were invited to social and celebratory events in the department, including those at my home. Some attended, some politely declined. I can imagine that some might have a rich enough social life outside the department that a faculty retirement party would not be appealing. But I think it was important that they were always invited.

Ten. Professional development opportunities may be seen as, and indeed are sometimes used as, a kind of indirect criticism. But workshops and seminars that help your staff to develop new skills and expertise can be a signal that you support them, and if

---

*Supervisors often take staff members out for lunch on Administrative Professionals Day—and depending on your relationship, your staff member(s) might really enjoy that. But they might prefer a gift card from the Olive Garden; I've worked with folks with whom a lunch would have seemed like some kind of punishment. At least beware of that possibility.

they are not used in a punitive way, staff may welcome them. Be on the lookout on your campus and beyond for opportunities for your staff partners to branch out and learn new skills, and of course give them the time away from the office that they'll need to attend and cover any costs of registration, travel, and materials they'll need. You'll do a better job of this—your gesture is more likely to be perceived as generous rather than critical—if you seek out opportunities that make the best use of their interests instead of simply considering your own needs. And ask your staff colleagues to bring professional development opportunities to you that they're interested in pursuing; the annual review is a natural time (among others) to raise the subject. If you're doing a good job of supporting your staff, they may well grow out of the job or the institution. A good chair doesn't hold back their staff so that they never fly the coop.

Supervising and supporting the work of staff colleagues can feel like quite a stretch to faculty members who are much more familiar with peer relationships. Without becoming the type of overbearing or micromanaging or egocentric boss you often see in sitcoms, though, you can create a mutually supportive working relationship with department staff that will provide professional satisfaction for them in their role and free you up to do what you do best in yours.

Chapter 5

Managing Resources

I'll now shift my focus from the role of chair as leader to that of manager. At its best, leadership is visionary: management is ordinary. Leadership is exciting (if often challenging), whereas management is sometimes mundane. But your department—its faculty and students and programs—cannot flourish unless those mundane details get taken care of.

Although it may not be the most important thing that you manage—you may manage staff members, for instance, and (in a very different sense) manage other resources such as office space or teaching assignments or logistical support for your faculty—the department's budget is the most visible—and the most symbolically charged—of its resources. In some departments where faculty and staff salaries and the wages of student workers are paid by academic affairs and discretionary spending is minimal, budget management is a small-dollar affair (but no less highly charged for all that); in other institutional contexts, a chair may be responsible for managing a significant discretionary budget.

I've had opportunities to manage at both ends of this continuum—a department with much and a department with little. Given human nature, it's perhaps not surprising that friction over the budget was greater where the budget was greater. At the poorer institution, faculty had grown accustomed over many years to doing more with less. A colleague used to joke that the messages we got from the upper administration were essentially what Pharoah told the Israelites: "More bricks, less straw." We didn't fight over money because there was almost no money to fight over. In that setting, it seemed important that nearly every fiscal decision involved other faculty members; in slicing up a very meager pie I didn't want to appear to be making capricious or nepotistic decisions. And unless yours is a small department with a tradition of making decisions by a committee of the whole or perhaps a department with enough resources to meet all demands, it's probably best to establish a budget committee you can consult with about these requests.

Even in a department with few discretionary resources, though, it's worth creating a floor for funding requests below which a chair can make an "executive decision" without consultation. That floor might be $50 in some departments and $500 in others, but there's a baseline beneath which it's not worth your colleagues' time (and the potential for conflict) to involve the department faculty. Think of these funds like the small awards that program officers at some granting agencies are able to make at their own discretion. The threshold for involving the department will of course depend on local circumstances and should be discussed with and agreed to by the department faculty. But setting a minimum that pushes funding requests to a faculty committee will ensure that those requests that must be deliberated on by your colleagues are at least worth their time.

Working with Budgets

If you hope to have your faculty colleagues trust you in your management of the budget, you'll need to have some big-picture discussions with them so they have a context for understanding the decisions that are being made. There are good reasons to keep the information you share with your colleagues within the department, so hold these conversations in confidence and collect any documentation after you share it in a meeting. Comparisons of resources between departments can be invidious, and in any event any discrepancies lie largely outside your control. In the years when I chaired a well-resourced department, we held at least two meetings each academic year devoted primarily to discussion of the budget. In the first, at the opening of the academic year, we reviewed the current year's budget in some detail, discussing our priorities for various categories of expense and making sure that everyone had a big-picture idea of what kinds of elective activities might be possible within our budget. Closely aligned with that first meeting and following just a couple of months later, we would meet when the call went out to departments to submit budgets for the upcoming year. This normally happened in the closing weeks of the fall semester, since budgets were due at the dean's office before the semester break.

One important decision you'll have to make when administering department funds is whether to have faculty requests submitted periodically (perhaps at the beginning of each term) or on a rolling basis. Each model has its advantages: collecting a number of requests at one time allows those involved in the decision to consider the relative strengths of each proposal in light of the funding available, but it disadvantages faculty who might become aware with short notice of an opportunity that doesn't align with the department's deadlines. With a bit of finesse you may be able to craft a compromise by making most of the discretionary budget available in two or three tranches during the academic year and holding aside a small pot for emergencies and short-notice opportunities. In some departments—laboratory sciences, for instance—this "rainy-day budget" may be quite significant for handling the needs of facilities and repairing or replacing equipment.

Sometimes my role as manager of the department budget meant that I had to play "bad cop." Even departments with significant restricted-funds budgets need to use those funds within the guidelines established by the institution. Obviously, research funds can't be used to pay for vacation travel, for instance, and purchases that might strike an approver up the line as lavish or extravagant need to be considered carefully. I had a colleague who was very generous by nature and liked to really "do things up right" when we entertained a visiting speaker. But the college has a per-person cap on restaurant meals. When a restaurant charge was refused at the dean's level, we would have to have a little talk; we had that talk more than once. It didn't matter that the department could afford it; college guidelines forbade it. It is sometimes useful, for this reason, to include the institution's strategic vision statement or documents in the discussion of the department's budget. Even when a department has "its own money," it can't always make all the decisions about how to spend that money.

Restricted versus Unrestricted Funds

Most academic departments operate on a budget made up of funds committed from the dean's office and some combination of donor-contributed and grant funding earmarked for the department (or individual faculty members and their research projects). In most administrative structures, the salaries of faculty, staff, and student workers are paid centrally by college or university administration. These lines are invisible to the department chair; they don't appear in their budget and the chair has no role in managing them (apart from possibly making recommendations about raises and other salary adjustments). Despite the push on many campuses for departments to become "entrepreneurial" by raising the funds necessary to support the department through donors and outside grants, internally allocated funds are the largest part of the budget for most departments. In humanities and social science departments especially, personnel costs account for the majority of costs and they're "off the books" as far as the department goes. Colleges and universities typically also fund at least some portion of faculty research and travel centrally and pay for utilities, building maintenance, and so forth. In theory, at least, the essential costs of delivering a college education are intended to be borne by the institution at large rather than by the departments.*

How much additional support beyond this core functional budget is available to departments and how much of it comes from the dean's office along with restricted funds† designated for the department's use varies greatly by institution. Some faculty enjoy unrestricted (if not completely unmonitored) photocopying privileges, for example; at some institutions, faculty must pay for their own. Back in the days when long-distance calling was a somewhat exotic thing, I taught at an institution where faculty had to put these charges on a personal credit card; at the next institution I worked for, I could simply direct dial such a call. Surely it is no great secret that the quality of life for faculty members (not to mention students and staff) differs greatly between our richest and leanest institutions. If you chair a department that is strapped for resources, you'll need to deal with the effects of

---

*At some public institutions over the past decades, however, this has become more the exception than the rule. A dean of mine at a public university would sometimes quip, "We're no longer state supported—only state located."

†Although there are some nuances here, I'm using the term "restricted funds" to refer to funding that arrives from sources other than the dean's office—usually funds given by donors or awarded by granting agencies that are restricted to purposes outlined in the gift language or the grant award. These funds cannot be transferred to other purposes or other units. "Unrestricted funds" are funds from the general college or university sources used to support your department.

that penury on your faculty colleagues. Conversely, if you're in a resource-rich department, you'll contend with challenges stemming from that affluence. The struggle for resources is a constant, irrespective of the resources available.

If you are fortunate enough to lead a department with a significant restricted-funds budget, though, you'll have some actual budget management work to do. Even at institutions that enjoy significant restricted funds, endowments can range from lavish to none between departments. Some departments will be sitting on pots of money, the product of a legacy of alumni giving that generates interest each year. In some cases, the money is earmarked for purposes that are no longer of interest to the department's faculty. Many institutions, for instance, have had to consider whether funds donated for books or department libraries could be interpreted to allow for the purchase of e-books or other forms of information technology (a subscription to a database, for instance). In extreme cases (for example, funds to endow a lecture series on a topic that is now obsolete), the institution may need to work with the trustees of the fund or go to court in order to have the money repurposed. In this scenario, your job as the chair of a department with significant endowed funds is to ensure that the annual interest on the endowment is used to support your faculty, students, and staff in keeping with the wishes of the donor as expressed in the gift agreement.

Meanwhile, it is in the interest of college or university administrators to level out inequities between academic units to the degree that it is possible to do so. A dean will not be thrilled if faculty in the anthropology department, for instance, can make three fully funded research trips each year using endowed department funds while members of the neuroscience department are lucky to have one trip reimbursed through the dean's office. Long-established departments are more likely to have accrued endowed funds than newer ones and some majors tend to produce graduates with higher lifetime earnings than others. One thing a dean can do in such a situation is require a generously endowed department to take on some part of the cost of its core operation—paying all or part of its staff salaries, for instance, or student wages or faculty research expenses. This frees up more of the dean's unrestricted funds that can be used to help less fortunate departments.

If your department is relatively richer than an adjacent discipline, you may be in a position to help support the programming of your less fortunate neighbor by (for instance) bearing the full cost of shared events or offering to co-sponsor programming that is of interest to the faculty of your department. Precisely because the legal language around restricted funds means that they're not fungible, they represent both a boon and a challenge—a boon to the lucky recipient, but something of a challenge to the cause of equity among disciplines and departments on campus. At an institution with significant restricted-funds budgets in some of the departments, finding ways to partner is a way of strengthening the scholarly community, whether you're the richer or poorer partner.

Keeping the Books

As I write in 2021, American colleges and universities are in the midst of a technological shift in the way campus finances are managed. Most institutions now use some kind of centralized financial and personnel management system. Workday, for instance, has been adopted on my campus and many other campuses.* When fully implemented, such systems promise to provide powerful budgeting and forecasting tools, along with expense reconciliation, payroll management, and employee timekeeping. Some critics, however, would suggest that full implementation is an ever-receding horizon. On my campus, where I am currently the director of a program, I need to use Workday to enter my ex-

---

*I was tempted to call Workday a popular management system, but it's far from popular, at least with faculty members on my campus.

penses, approve all the expenditures of my unit, and approve my staff colleague's biweekly timesheets. Workday pays no mind to weekends or holidays; alerts arrive at all hours informing me that I have expenses to approve. Indeed, an app on my phone means that I'm capable, in theory if not in spirit, of constant budget management. It can be exhausting. To make matters worse, real-time financial tracking still doesn't really function properly—and our funding is modest enough that I need frequent real-time checks on our expenditures.

For that reason, in my program we keep a shadow set of books in an Excel spreadsheet, although I know that this exasperates our finance office. Our finance folks frequently tell me that our centralized financial system can do everything for me that Excel can do, but that hasn't been my experience thus far and I feel more comfortable running my own numbers alongside the Workday system. When I assumed my first chair's position more than two decades ago, a working knowledge of Excel seemed to an English professor like an exotic finishing-school ornament, like skill in flower arrangement or ballroom dancing. Somewhere along the way, though, it became an essential proficiency for a department chair. I once was proud of my inability to use Excel, thinking it evidence of my resistance to being coopted by the educational-industrial complex. Now I'm able not only to read spreadsheets campus administrators send me but to create my own for both professional and personal purposes. (I've got Excel running in another window right now, open to a spreadsheet tracking my progress on completion of this manuscript.) It's a tool, and like all tools, it's entirely value neutral. Tame it: make it your friend. If your campus IT division doesn't conduct trainings in Excel, there are many free options available as YouTube videos—or just dive in and Google the problem you need to solve when your skills hit a roadblock.

As department chair, you will almost certainly be collaborating on budget management with a staff member—often someone who is much more adept in financial matters than you are. If you trust them, they can be a great ally. Having periodic conversations with your staff colleague and giving them opportunities to alert you to emerging situations can alleviate a great deal of financial noise from the picture, a picture you'd prefer to have dominated by the flourishing of your students and faculty. But you're the chair, and ultimately it's your signature that authorizes expenditures coming out of the department's unrestricted and (if applicable) restricted-funds budgets. You may be able to delegate some of the work, but you can't delegate the authority or the responsibility.

Managing Off-Budget Resources

Finally, in some institutional settings, the department chair is responsible for a couple of other kinds of resources that faculty care about a great deal: office, lab, and performance spaces; access to facilities; and salary increases. In some systems, the dean or provost manages space centrally and you'll have no formal role. But if your department does control some amount of campus real estate and it falls to you to make office assignments and reassignments, you'll need to work out a dispassionate system for allocating those spaces that doesn't hinge on your personal relationships with any of your faculty colleagues. (In departments with specialized facilities, such as science and performing arts departments, you may be working with a facilities manager.)

Fallible humans that we are, faculty members can read an implicit judgment on their performance and their value to the department into most any decision you make. Don't let space assignments be seen as a proxy for evaluation of merit. In the department where I now teach, we use seniority for many of these decisions. We know when each of us was hired, and those who have been here the longest get first pick when a new office space becomes available. (This is, for us, independent of rank: an associate professor who has been in the department longer than a full professor has seniority over them.) It's a bit of a ridiculous musical-chairs scenario, but available space is offered first to the most senior colleague, who either takes it or passes onto the next. If they take it, their office becomes available and is subject to the same lottery. In practice, it's not quite as chaotic as it sounds; senior faculty tend already to be installed in the more coveted spaces and their long residency acts as a disincentive to moving.

This brings up another point: why are buildings created with different-sized offices and lab spaces in the first place? My office building was built in the late nineteenth century, and although it has undergone periodic renovations, the basic architecture—some large corner offices with lots of windows but also some smaller, tighter, darker offices—is beyond the scope of a renovation to remediate. However, if you are in the position of overseeing a major building renovation during your time as chair, think about what can be done to make the work spaces of your colleagues (including staff) more equitable.

And then there are salaries. In a previous institution where I was chair, a small merit review committee evaluated each department faculty member each year, assigned points to each, and provided a ranking. Those rankings were then advisory to but not binding on me. The faculty union had created the system, and in principle, it promised to combine fairness with rigor in the evaluation of faculty performance. However, in practice, it managed to produce about as many happy outcomes as the Spanish Inquisition. Indeed, it seemed to have combined the worst features of every salary-setting mechanism I've ever heard of. The merit ratings took a great deal of faculty time to produce and at no small interpersonal cost, but the institution was quite poor, so someone with an excellent rating might end up with a raise of $35 per month more than someone at the bottom of the scale. As chair, I was shielded to some degree by the faculty committee that produced the rankings, but since they were only advisory, I was always held responsible if I didn't intervene to correct the injustice that a faculty colleague felt had been done them. Furthermore, since it was a public institution, all salaries were public and published, which only served to fuel faculty members' sense of unfairness. (To be sure, publishing salaries accomplishes other things too, including allowing faculty members to negotiate their own salaries with better information.)

Although chairs are stuck with the system that's in place, things are much simpler for a chair under the system where I teach now. As chair, I have no input into faculty raises: annual performance reviews go directly to the dean of the college, who sets salaries with the president. This system has the serious drawback that faculty members don't feel like they have an advocate in the process who understands their discipline and their research. It's all a bit of a black box: annual performance report in, annual salary letter out. But it does make life significantly simpler for the poor chair who under any system has very little control over colleagues' salaries but can serve as a lightning rod for their discontent just the same. Add to that the fact that I'm at a private institution and in more than a decade here, I've never known what a colleague was paid. I might be unhappy with my salary, but I don't feel underappreciated compared with Prof. Brown. (But the same proviso applies as above: since faculty salaries are private, individual faculty members don't have much leverage for arguing for an adjustment to their salary unless they voluntarily share those figures among themselves, which some do.)

Because chairs typically have little or no role in setting colleagues' salaries, their interests must be represented by the dean, even though those decisions can affect your work and the functioning of your department very directly. The first is in salary negotiations for a new hire. You can indicate your strong desire to hire a candidate to your dean, but they are going to do the research to determine an appropriate market salary, and they, not you, are going to negotiate with the candidate. When it's the dean's money, there's a temptation for departments to say, "give them whatever it takes!"—which is, perhaps, why chairs don't negotiate these deals. Besides putting a strain on the institution's resources, such myopic negotiations can result in new faculty coming in at higher salaries than some hardworking longtime colleagues, which creates a terrible environment within the department when the disparity comes to light (and it will).

A similar dynamic is in play when a colleague receives an offer from another institution and desires a counteroffer. Your dean will want to know whether, or how badly, you want to retain the colleague. If you have a good relationship with your colleague, they may well confide in you regarding the situation and perhaps ask you to weigh in with the dean. But here again, the dean is charged with working toward equity in faculty salaries and they are in a position to know the full salary landscape in detail, whereas you are not. If your colleague is of great value to your department you should be all means make the case as forcefully as you can for their retention, but after that, it's out of your hands.

Managing your department's resources isn't, I would argue, the most important thing you do as a chair. Many of the most significant things you can do to support your colleagues cost little or nothing and just require you to be alert to their needs and resourceful in your thinking. But the (sometimes rather small) budgets that we do control have a disproportionate symbolic weight. As chair, you'll need to be seen to manage your department's financial resources equitably while knowing that your real power to do good largely lies elsewhere.

Chapter 6

Stewarding the Department's Curricula

Although your department's faculty will be part of the discussions as your institution's general education requirements are put in place and periodically revised, once they've been implemented, yours is not to reason why—yours is just to do (or be defunded). To say it another way, when it comes to the general education curriculum, the department's role isn't to figure out *what* (though certainly it has a voice as the college decides this), but *how*. This area of the curriculum is put together with an eye toward the education of students in general rather than that of the students concentrating in your field.

In contrast, the department's disciplinary programs—its major or majors, which may have multiple tracks or emphases; its minor or minors; and other kinds of diploma or certification opportunities—are where the department declares itself regarding its field of study and determines what an educated student with the department's name highlighted on their diploma ought to know about it. Even that task is open to interpretation, of course. In a chemistry department, for instance, the argument might be made that the major curriculum should prepare a student in one or more of these ways: prepare them for successful graduate study in chemistry and related fields; prepare them to undertake work as a chemist in the private sector or at a not-for-profit; enable them to critically read new research being produced in the field; allow them to go on, with appropriate credentialing, to teach the subject to primary or secondary school students; or even provide a basic kind of "chemical literacy" that will allow them to be an informed, literate citizen, able to (for instance) assess competing scientific claims on an issue of public importance such as climate change and public health. Where a department lands in this matrix of possibilities will depend on variables like institutional identity, history, and mission, and the scholarly interests and ambitions of its faculty.

Framing the Curriculum

In all likelihood, during your term as chair you will not be called upon to oversee the creation of a new major from scratch; these are once-in-a-lifetime events in the history of a department. However, a major is something of a living curriculum, subject to the changing state of the field, the expertise of the department's faculty, and the interests of its students. Revision should be discussed periodically, and such revision can even encompass the creation of a new, complementary major within the department as the field expands.

Even though the curriculum is the one area where all faculty should be able to pull together in the interest of their students, these conversations can be difficult and contentious. There is something of a tendency—which we're always on our guard against and work valiantly to avoid—to reflexively replicate in our own departments the curricula we studied as undergraduates and graduate students (while taking the opportunity, perhaps, to eliminate aspects of our own training that struck us as irrelevant or oppressive). Which is to say that without careful scrutiny, our curricula can simply (often unconsciously) replicate the strengths while avoiding what we perceive to have been the weaknesses of the programs we were credentialed in. It's a bit like parenting, perhaps: new parents often report their surprise at discovering the ways their own parenting unconsciously echoes the rearing they received, even when they have vowed not to repeat patterns or values from their upbringing that they found harmful. Instead of being thoughtful and creative, our curricula can become flatly reactive.

At least I recognize these impulses in myself. My PhD is in a field that I added as a second major at the eleventh hour as an undergraduate. Because the clock was ticking and I had the support of faculty members who wanted to help me, the department waived some requirements in the major for me—in particular, the yearlong survey of British literature. As a result—not having taken the course but worrying constantly during the forty years since that skipping it has been holding me back in numerous untold ways—I made a fetish of it. In my first (non-tenure-track) position, I was assigned to teach the second semester of the course, which provoked an undue amount of anxiety. It also forced me to do a lot of filling in, which has stood me in good stead ever since. At institutions where I've taught, I've argued (albeit unsuccessfully) for it to be added to majors that lacked it, even as the field of literary studies has been moving away from the somewhat quixotic notion of "field coverage." Indeed, in a development my undergraduate self never could have imagined, I ended up as the general editor of a 6,000-page British literature anthology, the textbook for precisely those courses I had ducked out of.

This story points up one of the psychic advantages of reproducing the curricula with which we were trained: such curricula center us, making our experience normative, the standard by which achievement in the field should be measured. (Not insignificantly, they also ensure that new course preparation can be kept to a minimum.) Had I succeeded in creating any of the major curricula I've taught in after my own image, I would also have succeeded in training cohorts of students for a degree conferred on me in 1981. As chair, your role is to rise above these personal predilections—both those of your colleagues and your own—and be the spokesperson for a major that reflects the current realities of your field, the lives of your students, the real world (or further academic study) into which they'll be emerging, and the expertise and interests of your faculty. You're there, in part, to make conscious the subconscious and unconscious subtexts of these discussions, making sure that curricular decisions answer to externalities rather than to internalized notions of the curriculum that haven't been tested against current realities.

What should dictate the shape of a departmental curriculum, be that the requirements for a major, a minor, a certificate, or an emphasis? Majors (to use the most common example) are typically reverse engineered, often with imperfect information. But normally, whether consciously or not, we think about what we want our students to know at the end of their degree program, what competencies they will have, what disciplinary knowledge they will command—and then think backward about the sequence of courses that will get them to that point. In some disciplines, outside bodies (professional organizations, accreditors, licensing bodies) provide suggestions or even requirements that must be met. Even in these situations, though, there's some room left for electives and coursework through which a department can leave its individual stamp.

Although new developments in the discipline are the primary source of curricular innovation, another impetus is closer to hand: the nature of institution in which you work, the mission of that institution, and new initiatives in allied departments. For example, the consortium my college is a member of is adding a medical school. What opportunities might that create for English and for the humanities center I now direct? Medical humanities is a growing area at institutions across the country, even at liberal arts colleges like ours. Might one or both of the units I'm associated with attract students if I and my colleagues think about new programming that would connect us with health care fields?

Major curricula are often divided into the two broad groups of vertical and horizontal curricula. As a broad generalization, the STEM disciplines create vertical curricula, while the humanities disciplines are horizontal (with some exceptions; for instance, foreign languages). A vertical curriculum requires not only that certain courses be completed for the major but also that they be completed for the most part in a certain sequence: single-variable calculus precedes multivariable calculus, which is a prerequisite for linear algebra; general chemistry precedes organic and physical chemistry; intermediate Spanish is required for advanced Spanish. Horizontal majors impose fewer constraints on the order in which students take their required courses. After an introductory course that offers an overview of the field and its methods, some departments will allow sociology majors, for example, to take courses in the major as fancy moves them. Neither model is "right," of course. The structure of knowledge is arguably more hierarchical in some disciplines than others. However, a vertical curriculum imposes greater demands on the department that offers it: if Bio 1 is a prerequisite for Bio 2 and Bio 2 is offered only once a year, then the department has an obligation to offer sufficient seats in Bio 1 every term so that students who want to make their way through the sequence in good time aren't impeded. And horizontal curricula risk downplaying the importance of preparatory courses and learning by pretending that any way into the major is as good as any other. Perhaps an art history course on Postimpressionism doesn't require the seminar on Impressionism as a prerequisite, but it's hard to believe that students who move from the latter to the former don't have an advantage.

In some situations, this curricular imperative can be both an advantage and a burden to departments. A department that petitions to hire a temporary faculty member to fill in during the absence of a colleague who teaches a prerequisite in the major sequence, for instance, has a stronger argument for the position than a department that does not offer any courses that must be offered in any given semester. If the course the latter department is seeking an instructor for isn't offered next term, a dean or provost can reasonably suggest, students can take it the following term.

A Curriculum and Its Faculty

And this brings up the final point to be made about curricular planning in the department context. The relationship between a department's curriculum and its faculty is dynamic. And while for the sake of discussion, it's easiest to posit discrete moments of curricular study and revision, a healthy department engages in low-stakes conversations about the curriculum on a regular basis, just as it does in discussions of diversity, equity, and inclusion or of safety concerns in the lab sciences.

But imagine for a moment that you're going to lead your department in a discussion about revising the major. Will you plan for curricular changes and new courses based on the expertise already in the department? If so, you'll be limited in how much you can change: if your history department doesn't have a scholar working in digital humanities, you're not going to be able to create a vibrant quantitative methods track within the major. By the same token, if you don't allow your reach as a department to exceed your grasp—if the extent of curricular reform is limited to the teaching expertise that's already in the department—it's hard to see how the curriculum can ever be anything but backward looking. In a department that trains graduate students and involves them in its teaching mission, there may be some possibility of bringing their cutting-edge work into the course offerings, although planning a major based on the availability of such courses would be risky. Postdoctoral fellows, if your department has an opportunity to host them, may be able to add a new course to broaden the department's offerings. But again, these opportunities probably aren't reliable enough to build a curriculum around.

This presents a seeming catch-22 to departments engaged in curricular revision. Should they restrict the curriculum to what can be taught by existing faculty or should they attempt to leverage curricular reform to create new faculty positions? I would suggest that the first of these options is always available to you and your colleagues—that is to say, it should be your fallback position. The more important conversation to engage—the thought experiment that can prove motivating and even visionary for your department, even if you end up at the fallback position—is about what you'd like your curriculum to look like without prematurely bringing constraints to bear on the conversation. Call it a blue-sky exercise: if the department were to write its curriculum now without regard to its history or the limitations of current staffing, what would members feel excited about offering?*

If your blue-sky plan is to move from the safe confines of your department's conference space and make its way through the institution's approval structures, you will need to strategize carefully and you must have full buy-in from your department colleagues. The plan must create a vision that is compelling to those outside your department whose approval will be required, including college-wide curriculum and/or new-position committees, the full college faculty, and the dean and/or the provost. Such a plan will be strengthened by outside validation, either through comparison to the curricula at peer institutions or suggestions made in the report of outside reviewers (or both).

---

*While it should prove freeing to think without worrying about current holes in faculty expertise, it's probably not productive to imagine the size of the faculty growing exponentially. If yours is a department of 20, you might think about what specializations could be added with a retirement or two down the road and/or the granting of a new position to the department. It probably doesn't make sense to imagine suddenly gaining half a dozen new faculty lines.

Delivering the Curriculum

Years ago I was invited to teach a course as a visiting professor in a graduate program. I was open to the idea, so I immediately asked the department chair who had phoned me, "What do you need?" By which I meant, What course needs to be offered that isn't being offered? What do your students need in order to make progress toward their degrees? What is the temporary hole in your curriculum that you need me to fill?

The answer that came back surprised me so much that I remember it more than a decade later: "You can teach whatever you want." As we talked more, I came to understand that the program in question was in real financial/staffing straits and the chair didn't feel that they could afford to be picky: what they needed was precisely any graduate-level course in English. And that I could do. The story has a happy ending: I had a graduate-level seminar in mind that I was happy to teach, and it (coincidentally) nicely complemented other recent offerings in the department. The course made sense for me and for the students, but by happy accident, not by design.

But the story illustrates, I think, the role department chairs play in scheduling course offerings and overseeing the curriculum. In this anecdote, both of the principals were department chairs (I was chairing my own department at the time), but while I was cast in the role of instructor, I was the one who approached the situation thinking like a chair. To be fair, I now know that the chair who reached out to me was in no position to be finicky; owing to institutional circumstances beyond their control, they weren't really able to do their job in a fully thoughtful way. As chair, part of your charge is to balance the teaching desires of your faculty colleagues against the curricular needs of your students. In a system in which two parties with at least partially opposing needs are contesting to get those needs met (students who need for a fundamentally solid curriculum in their major course of study and offerings to satisfy general education requirements and faculty who seek courses in which they can exercise and deepen their expertise), you've been appointed the referee.

A situation that's tipped too far to either side—with course offerings dictated exclusively either by curricular requirements or by the research agendas of faculty—won't ultimately work well for either party. Faculty who have earned terminal degrees with specific research interests won't thrive if their teaching assignments never allow them to tap into their expertise and passion, and as a result, their students may suffer through merely dutiful teaching. But by the same token, faculty who teach only advanced courses in their research specialties to students who haven't been taught the fundamentals of the discipline and thus are not properly prepared for them won't reach those students and won't be happy with the results. For this reason, most departments have guidelines, or at least informal conventions, that distribute a faculty member's teaching between introductory and advanced courses. This has the benefit of offering faculty members a varied teaching assignment that includes at least occasional advanced courses and providing courses up and down the curriculum for students.

While most would agree that all faculty members should be involved in both teaching some general education and non-major courses and with delivering the curriculum for departmental majors while also enjoying opportunities to teach in their specialty areas, the devil is in the details. At one institution where I taught, assistant professors were required to teach half of their courses (three courses of a six-course annual load) in the "service" curriculum—in our case, first-year composition. With promotion to associate professor, that service obligation was reduced to two courses annually; with promotion to professor, one. Such a rank-based system wouldn't be to every department's liking; certainly it ran against my egalitarian streak. But some formalized system that is known to all the affected parties and is fairly administered is essential.

Achieving this balance for faculty members and students can be a real challenge for a department that's positioned within its institution as a service department. In practice, departments are never officially referred to this way: "service department" is a functional description that designates a unit whose focus isn't central to the institution's mission (a studio art department in an engineering school, for instance) and whose role is to provide breadth courses to students whose primary interests lie elsewhere. And because the focus of a two-year college is normally either vocational training or preparation for transferring to a four-year institution, all liberal arts departments at those institutions function as service departments in a sense and faculty may have few opportunities to teach in the areas that led them to graduate study.

When I was in graduate school, the professor who became my dissertation director would send around a memo the term before they were scheduled to teach a graduate seminar asking all prospective students what work they'd most like to do with them. They'd present a few possibilities—we could study X, Y, or Z—and then would offer the seminar that promised to be most helpful to the largest number of students. (A crucial, and related, question, my director would never have thought to ask their students would have been "And how should I teach it?") Not all of our colleagues will readily adopt such a collegial attitude toward their teaching, but appealing to the needs of the students we share is a chair's best way to make the case.

Of course, as a department chair, one is incredibly grateful for faculty colleagues who are happy to teach where they're needed, and the best way to cultivate such generosity is to display it yourself when you're not in the chair's role. It has perhaps been easier for me than some, since I rarely find classes in my specialties to be genuinely synergistic with my research, although I enjoy teaching them. I find that teaching an intro course or a course for non-majors is just as conducive to my writing productivity as an advanced seminar designed to explore precisely the topic of my current research. Not everyone, I realize, feels that way. (For some of my colleagues in the sciences, the notion of synergy between teaching and research is rather fanciful, especially when teaching undergraduates. For them, the best fit would involve choosing courses that better prepare students to engage with them in their scholarship.)

Likewise, chairs are grateful for faculty members who don't bring inflexible constraints to course scheduling. Here too, some of us can afford to be more generous and flexible, some less so. Some of us are struggling to maintain a complex work-life balance that involves caring for young children or aging parents or facing a time-consuming commute, for example. None of these have been factors for me for the past decade and more, so I've been able to tell my chair to schedule me where it works the best and leave the most sought-after time slots and weekly schedules to those who truly need them.

Administering Transfer Credit

In some department structures—those without an undergraduate director, for instance—it falls to the chair to evaluate credits that students want to transfer in from another institution. Whether or not outside credits are accepted by your institution is a question the institution itself decides and is normally tracked by the registrar's office. But whether a particular course from an accredited institution counts as a course in your department, a course within the major, or a replacement for a particular course is a decision for the department faculty, and that decision is often delegated to the chair. At some institutions where I have worked, articulation agreements were in place that stipulated the transfer equivalency for a great number of courses offered at other institutions within the state system. If a student took a literature course at a local community college, for instance, there was nothing for me to adjudicate—the transfer equivalencies were worked out cooperatively with faculty from the peer institutions, they were recorded centrally, and the student's transcript was updated automatically.

If such an agreement is not in place, a department chair (or delegated colleague or department committee) goes through an equivalent process. At my current institution, we do not have standing transfer arrangements in place. If a student presents a credit from another institution—or confers with the department chair prior to taking the course in order to have the course pre-approved—the chair will look at a catalog description (or a course syllabus if it is available) to determine whether the content and level make course credit in the home department appropriate. Then the registrar's office will be able to provide course-credit equivalencies when converting from one academic term (semesters, quarters, trimesters) to another. Determining whether a course the institution accepts for transfer credit should count as an English course (in my case) is relatively straightforward. Deciding whether it should count toward completion of the major, on the other hand—whether as a required course in the major or as an elective credit—requires more careful calibration to your department's requirements and offerings. (The same is true for study abroad courses, and if your institution sends many students abroad, you or your colleagues will spend a good deal of time with those students advising them about which courses will fit well into the major.) The departments I've taught in have tended to be fairly flexible about elective credits unless it's a course that doesn't meet the minimum learning objectives for our departmental offerings (such as, in our case, a developmental writing course). The fact that a particular course isn't available at my institution is no reason for rejecting it—indeed, that may be precisely the reason that a student sought it out. But if it doesn't meet the standards for college-level work as understood in my department, that's when the veto pen might come out.

Ultimately, as the arc of this chapter demonstrates, the curriculum as an abstract set of courses or requirements is not cleanly separable from the students who undertake it and the faculty who teach it. In at least one of its aspects, the curriculum is an inter-face between students and faculty that facilitates transformative (and sometimes lifelong) relationships. (I had an email recently from a former student I haven't heard from in fifteen years. He's now a professor at a university in Egypt, the country of his birth, and he wrote to invite me to join the editorial board of a journal he's editing.) We put our curricula together and revise them in order to represent the current understanding of our fields and to train students in our disciplines for fulfilling lives after college, whether they use their disciplinary training or not. But in teaching those curricula, we also attract and connect with students who share our excitement for the material and with whom some-times deep and durable relationships. That's part of what a cur-riculum does, too.

Chapter 7

Highlighting the Big Picture in Planning

All but the newest, most recently created departments have a store of traditions, ways they've always done things. That is to say, they benefit from some momentum: the faculty and staff could, if the need arose, run on "muscle memory" for a period of time. In large part this is a very good thing: if we know that we always buy our copier paper from Acme Office Supply, that's one less detail to fret over, and if Prof. Wang always teaches on Tuesdays and Thursdays, that's one less variable to consider in the complicated process of course planning. But of course, habits can be deadening as well as liberating and can prevent us from responding appropriately to the changing contexts of our work. What if Pine Mills now provides better paper at a better price and Prof. Wang's inflexible schedule is now riding roughshod over the needs of their colleagues?

Fortunately, a handful of formal opportunities for self-reflection are built into the structure and traditions of even the most hidebound departments. Departmental self-study and review are carried out at regular intervals (often on a 10-year cycle) under the auspices of a dean's or provost's office with the participation of a team of outside reviewers. I will address these institutionally mandated opportunities for reflection in chapter 10. In this chapter, I'll discuss opportunities that are closer to hand for a department chair and more open to their own shaping: department meetings and annual (or biannual) retreats. I'll discuss ways to make these exercises the most productive in helping a department meet its current needs and plan for the future.

Before I look at these formal occasions for the exchange of ideas, however, I want to discuss the most common planning and consensus-building activity of them all: simply hanging out in the department, having conversations, poking your head in to say hello as you walk by a colleague's open office door, making small talk around the copy machine or water cooler. We move work along when we plan for it in scheduled conversations, to be sure, but we also move things forward sometimes just by seizing the moments that come our way. The personal relationships that develop in a more informal setting can help facilitate the sometimes bureaucratic processes of formal departmental decision making.

However, there is a danger here: this style is informal, yes, but it's also potentially prejudiced or prejudicial. The colleague who invites you into their office is creating a private audience with the chair and special pleading can be the result. The information (or opinion) a chair gains in these one-on-one encounters always needs to be verified and triangulated with the input of the department as a whole. I remember trying to forge these personal connections when I took over my first chair's job. I was coming into a new department (and university) from another institution and I wanted to get to know everyone—their histories, their stories, their dreams, their lingering frustrations. So I made appointments to take each faculty colleague to lunch over the course of the first year. I certainly learned a lot and I hoped that everyone felt heard, but at times I thought my brain would explode as it tried to reconcile the frankly incommensurable accounts of department history and long-standing feuds I was taking in. Think of Akira Kurosawa's *Rashomon* or William Faulkner's *As I Lay Dying*: everyone was offering me puzzle pieces, but they often seemed to belong to different puzzles.

Nuts and Bolts of the Department Meeting

The formal gathering that under normal circumstances carries the lowest stakes (and occurs most frequently) is the department meeting. Even typing that phrase engenders a nervous flutter: department meetings, understandably the object of many jokes (such as the bingo card for the first faculty meeting of the year that McSweeney's published),* aren't anyone's favorite part of the scholarly life. At best, they're focused, brisk, and efficient while still allowing for substantive dialogue about important issues in the life of the department; at worst, they're characterized either by personal animus or tedium. I'll take up the risk of personal animus and how to deal with it in the next chapter; it is, to a large extent, beyond your control as chair (although you can help set boundaries for it). If a department meeting is tedious, though, that's on you.

Ensuring that a department meeting is productive and encouraging rather than enervating begins with good planning. Departmental bylaws (or just unwritten custom) will probably mandate that an agenda be circulated among the voting faculty of the department, often a day or two in advance of the meeting. (Some institutions and departments include contingent faculty and/or staff in these meetings; you'll want to be sensitive to local traditions when convening your meetings.) Although as chair you'll have the primary input into the contents and order of the agenda,

*Lisa Nikolidakis, "First Faculty Meeting of the Year Bingo," McSweeney's Internet Tendency, August 25, 2015, https://www.mcsweeneys.net/articles/first -faculty-meeting-of-the-year-bingo.

you'll want to invite suggestions for items from faculty colleagues. It's best to give them two or three days before the agenda needs to be finalized for distribution.

In a large department or even a small department with busy faculty pulled in many different directions, finding a meeting time that works for everyone can be a challenge. Meetings at the end of the teaching day might mean that there are no teaching conflicts, but they can make it difficult for colleagues who have young children or other family obligations or those who have significant commutes to participate fully. Sometimes early mornings are relatively clear times for a meeting, but some colleagues, like many students, find anything scheduled before 10 a.m. barbaric. Some departments thread the needle by scheduling department meetings during the lunch hour—everyone's got to eat, right?— and encouraging faculty to bring their lunch to the meeting (or, if the budget allows, occasionally providing a light lunch). Early in my career I taught in a department that by tradition had an hour blocked out in the weekly schedule when no one was allowed to teach, an hour that was therefore known to be available for department meetings and other events. Some colleges and universities build such a space into the weekly instructional calendar. Such an arrangement would not work well in all departments, but it might be worth considering.

Given the inevitable scheduling constraints, it's unlikely you'll be able to hold a meeting that lasts longer than an hour. At my institution, we do our best to squeeze our meetings into the 12:15-1:15 p.m. break in the teaching schedule for lunch, but meetings are always less than an hour because people coming from class arrive late and people who teach at 1:15 need to leave early. Depending on what's going on in the life of the department, an hour might not be very much time and you may need to make up for the limited duration of meetings by meeting more frequently. One department on my campus with an especially complicated schedule of public programming to coordinate meets for an hour every week (and at 8:00 a.m. to boot); some departments manage well by meeting for just an hour once a month. For some time, my department has been in the habit of meeting for an hour every other week, and if there is no time-critical business (relating to faculty hiring or tenure/promotion decisions, for example), that has usually seemed enough. Your department will have some tradition regarding the frequency of faculty meetings. My experience suggests that although it's a simple thing to convene them less frequently (no one will complain about fewer meetings), increasing their frequency is a tough sell.

All that describes the department meeting from the outside. Let's now enter the seminar room or private departmental space and look at the meeting from the inside. Your faculty colleagues have started to arrive. Some have printed out the agenda you circulated in advance and some will have taken out their laptops or tablets and pulled up an electronic copy, but it's still a good idea to have some printed copies available for those who arrive without unless you meet in a space that will allow you to project it. Given the decentralized nature of faculty work, the department meeting may be one of the few times when some colleagues see one another, so ideally there will be a few moments for greetings and small talk before you call the meeting to order.

Normally the first order of business is to accept the minutes of the previous meeting. This assumes, of course, that those minutes have been circulated in advance (although experience suggests that few will have read them). It also assumes that someone has been charged with taking the meeting minutes. In some departments, a staff member (such as an administrative assistant) may attend faculty meetings and be asked to take and circulate the minutes; in other departments, no staff members are in attendance, in which case it's often the practice that faculty members take turns with this task. Instead of asking for volunteers—which implicitly puts pressure on your junior colleagues to step up— consider asking your most senior colleague to start the rotation and work your way from most to least senior. It's a good idea to exempt yourself from the rotation since you're responsible for keeping the meeting moving; it's difficult for most of us to anticipate where the conversation needs to go and how to get there while recording where it's just been.

Typically, items that are more time sensitive or more important are front loaded in the meeting agenda. In part, this is a nod to the possibility that not everything on the agenda can be covered in the time available. It's customary to close with an opportunity for faculty members to bring new business (if only to have it added to the agenda for the next meeting) and a time for announcements of coming events. I always conclude my printed agendas with the date and time of the next department meeting.

The Department Meeting and Its Discontents

That's the bare outline of a department meeting, and there's nothing very controversial in what I've said so far. Some years ago I gave a workshop at an Association of Departments of English summer seminar for department chairs on how to run an effective department meeting and started the time we had together by asking the group, "Why do we hate department meetings?" The responses might provide a useful framework for thinking about meeting dynamics. Here's the shorthand version of the list we came up with that afternoon. I'll try to unpack as we go along.

1. Length/scheduling
2. Dominant voice
3. What's the purpose?
4. Lack of direction, focus, or productive conversation
5. Meeting-to-meeting continuity and follow-through

I've already said something about point 1. I'll add that a department needs to consider what, if any, accommodations will be made for faculty members who are unable to attend a meeting. As I write this, COVID-19 has forced many of us for the past year and more to rely on electronic platforms such as Zoom for our teaching and other communications with students and colleagues.

This experience suggests that it will be possible, moving forward, to allow remote participation in department meetings. During the pandemic, many of us witnessed increased attendance at both college-wide and department meetings when they were held virtually. In my experience, it also seems that some colleagues feel freer to participate under these conditions.

Some would argue that having one or two colleagues "phone it in" while most of the faculty are present in a room is a terrible dynamic. I've experienced it and it's not ideal, to be sure. And if the research on teaching is applicable here, it's possible that hybrid delivery (in-person meeting with some remote participation) has rather poor outcomes. But especially in a small department, the alternative may be that faculty colleagues feel disenfranchised through no fault of their own and may resist any decisions made in their absence. Experienced faculty members will recognize that there's a fine line to be walked here: while we may believe that a colleague shouldn't be shut out from decision-making owing to the vagaries of scheduling, this must not be allowed to descend into a situation where faculty members refuse their responsibility to participate in departmental decision-making, then protest about the outcome. I've sometimes grimly joked that for some colleagues, "academic freedom" seems to mean the freedom to boycott the process and protest the outcome. But it's meant to be a joke, and an informed policy on absentee or remote participation in faculty meetings (including voting) must distinguish between planned, unavoidable absence and the flouting of faculty responsibilities.

I suspect that the simple phrase "dominant voice" in the list above communicates its intention quite clearly to anyone with much experience in any kind of group setting. Although many faculty colleagues are introverts (the long and lonely process of earning a PhD, at least in some disciplines, to some extent selects against those who thrive on interpersonal interaction), some of us sure like to hear our own voices when we gather to talk with colleagues. Sometimes it's the most senior voice in the room, the person who has been in the department longest and is most familiar (and perhaps most attached to) its traditions. Sometimes a bit of humorous teasing can set things right without embarrassing your voluble colleague. ("Bill, I'm *shocked* that you have something to add!") This won't work for everyone and it won't work all the time for anyone. This is tricky territory where prescriptions are of limited use, but by letting your alpha colleague dominate the conversation, you're not creating a safe space in which your less dominant (or just more circumspect) and often more vulnerable colleagues can be heard. It's a dynamic that will be familiar to all teachers from the classroom setting, and sometimes the strategies that work there will work for the faculty meeting as well, with some adjustments. For instance, some students don't so much want to push an agenda as they want or need to be heard. They're just as happy, or even happier, to have your one-on-one attention out of class and then don't need to commandeer it in class. Likewise, sometimes a private conversation with a faculty colleague can give them the chance they need to make their point of view known. When trying to reach consensus on an important question, sometimes it's effective to go around the meeting room systematically to create space for everyone to speak (without, of course, forcing anyone to do so). Make sure not to let the dominant voice have the last word.

Some colleges and universities, especially those that grew out of the Quaker tradition, hew to a carefully defined model of consensus decision-making in which "unity, not unanimity" is the goal. Instead of having a majority position triumph over a minority position after a faculty vote, all members of the decision-making body (in this case, the department) seek to find common ground, to persuade one another, and to come up with a solution that's acceptable to all. The process is not complete until the group has reached consensus. In the academic setting, while this might work well for some departments, it's also ripe for abuse. I've been party to "consensus" decision-making in which the minority position (in one case, a minority of one, who was also the department's "dominant voice") uses its objection to bring decision-making to a standstill. In the Quaker model, a person with a minority view may either "stand aside"—that is, note their disagreement but then allow the process to move forward—or "block," signaling that their opposition to the majority's proposal is unalterable. In some faculty settings, the only minority option seems to be to block. My experience with consensus decision-making may not be representative, but what I've seen makes me skeptical about its practicality in an academic setting.

Nothing is more demoralizing than a department meeting for the sake of a department meeting—a meeting after which your colleagues leave asking themselves (or worse, asking you) "What was the point?" Your colleagues are busy people; you're a busy person. You had better have a good reason to put an hour's embargo on everyone's schedule and bring them together. "It's been two weeks since our last meeting" is not a good reason. Think of the popular meme: "This meeting could have been an email." If your own sense as chair is that there isn't much to discuss for an upcoming scheduled meeting and if, after soliciting agenda items, nothing urgent comes back, that's when you should give your colleagues the gift of their hour back.

Which raises the question of how, or whether, to conduct what might otherwise qualify as department-meeting business by email. Faculty as a group don't love administrative email, but if a time-sensitive question can easily be resolved via email and save a department meeting, I'm grateful for that email. A chair needs to develop a sense of which questions are well suited to airing via email and which should be held for in-person meetings. The asynchronous nature of "Reply: All" can, for instance, mean that a question has effectively been decided by the time a colleague comes out of their afternoon class and they might rightly feel that their input has been bypassed. At one end of the spectrum, many simple logistical questions—choosing dates and times for departmental events, pro forma approval of small budget requests—are quickly managed in an email (or a polling/calendaring tool such as Doodle). At the other end, any conversations of a sensitive nature—such as those surrounding faculty hiring, staff evaluations, and tenure/promotion deliberations—must be handled in person under conditions of confidentiality. Remember, too, that while we're often unsuccessful in changing the minds of our colleagues in department meetings, there can be something serendipitous about the process: real-time conversations with colleagues can sometimes move hearts and minds in a way that the best of emails never will.

If you make sure that each department meeting that you convene has a purpose, you shouldn't have any trouble with the next item on our list, lack of focus or lack of direction in the meeting itself. If the meeting lacks focus, that's a function of the agenda, although it's often the case that regularly scheduled department meetings have several foci as the department seeks to move forward on a handful of issues at once. Lack of direction in a meeting is arguably something somewhat different. As chair, it's your unenviable job to make sure that the conversation stays on track and is productive. Unless you're combative by nature, it may feel uncomfortable, but your colleagues are counting on you to interrupt digressive commentary with the suggestion to move on or a promise to "put a pin in it" and bring it back for further discussion at another time or follow up with a colleague privately. Again, you'll endeavor to do this without embarrassing your colleagues, just as you gently redirect class conversation from a monologuing student.

What should your response be if a meeting concludes and you feel that the conversation has not been a productive one? A meeting can be unproductive in so many different ways. Most often, I'd guess, it's owing to a lack of preparation on the convener's part. If the issues under consideration require particular background, that context must be presented to those attending, either during the meeting or in materials that are distributed and read before the meeting. As department chair, it's easy to underestimate how much time may be needed to bring your colleagues up to speed on the background for a particular question. Because you're involved in conversations with your director, dean, or provost, you're spending more of your work week thinking about the larger contexts for some of these questions than your faculty colleagues are. If you've sat through a two-hour presentation regarding the roles of departments in the upcoming accreditation review, it's reasonable to hope that you can give your department colleagues the relevant background in less than two hours—but it's not reasonable (or at least not realistic) to imagine that most of them have any real interest, any real stake, in the institution's accreditation review. You are the bridge between the department and the institution's higher administration and are often the only one in your department who is paying attention to those higher-level conversations on campus. If your department is to participate meaningfully in those conversations (and you want it to), you'll need to provide the context for them.

One thing that can spoil an otherwise very productive meeting is a lack of continuity between meetings. An hour of conversation once or twice (or even four times) a month may be enough time to flesh out ideas and plans, but it's certainly not enough time to put them into action. That action needs to happen between meetings. For your faculty colleagues, department meetings exist as discrete, largely unwelcome interruptions to their teaching, research, and creative activity, not to mention their lives outside work. It's unrealistic for a chair to expect them to keep the issues that are raised in these meetings in the front of their minds in the time between them. No; that's your job. One common way to do this is with action items: concluding the discussion of each agenda item by asking (whether mentally or conversationally), "What work needs to be done to move this forward?" It might be research (into internship possibilities for your students); it might be a phone call (to the dean's office to confirm the due date for leave requests); it might be an email (to the chair of another department to inquire about their openness to cross-listing a course with your department next semester). Even though my execution is imperfect, I try to make sure each agenda item is paired with a between-meeting action item, if needed, and that each department meeting concludes with a rehearsal of the various action items we've agreed to as a group and who has agreed to take the next step on each. (These assignments, of course, should be captured in the meeting minutes.) And then—critically—these action items and any movement toward addressing them must be migrated to the agenda for the next meeting.

Another means of keeping track of departmental policy decisions, of course, is a department handbook of some kind. If you're lucky, you'll inherit such a document and will be responsible only for maintaining and updating it. In a worst-case scenario you may be in the position of seeing that one is created during your term, probably by brainstorming with your faculty (perhaps during a retreat) about its coverage and then assigning working groups to draft the various sections. This, along with other important departmental documents (tenure and promotion guidelines, learning objectives, program-review documents, budgets, etc.) should be saved in a networked space that current (and future) faculty have access to.

Departmental Retreats

Department meetings during the teaching term are a way to address issues as they arise during the school year and to keep some forward momentum for work that's under way in the department. If they are properly planned, they are normally spent doing meaningful work. But typically they're too brief to do big, long-term planning—the kind of conversations that are necessary to map out curricular reform, for instance, or plan for anticipated hires in the coming years. For those conversations to play out fully and without interruption, the best setting is a department retreat.

If the phrase "department meeting" strikes dread into the hearts of faculty members, "retreat" may generate an even stronger response—and make them want to do just that (retreat). For while department meetings can sometimes seem tedious or frustrating, at least they're brief and take place while faculty are "on the clock." A retreat, on the other hand, is most effective when it's scheduled for a full day (or almost a full day), takes place off campus, and happens outside the regular schedule. The potential gains are great, but it's also a big ask.

So a retreat can be a tough sell. How best to make the case to your colleagues? Well, if a daylong meeting is the only way to set an agenda for the year, the lack of such an agenda should be troubling your colleagues just as much as it is bothering you. Over time, it should be apparent that you've got a retreat-sized hole in your planning. If you have the resources, you can make the prospect more appealing by catering a light breakfast, a lunch, and/or a reception or a happy hour at the end of the day to wind down. This needn't be expensive, and if you conclude the day with a social hour at a bar or restaurant near your retreat site, colleagues can be asked to pay for their own refreshments. I've come to think that it's imperative to hold the retreat outside the normal work venue; there's something about being off site that frees people up to think differently about familiar issues and questions. Again, such a location need not be exotic or expensive; depending on the size of the department, meeting in one of your faculty member's homes (or your own) can serve well.

A retreat is a large container—that's the point—and it can hold a lot. But what it's really designed for is not a large number of small topics but a small number of big projects, big conversations, big decisions. Your regular department meetings can handle the small stuff; a retreat is where you set an agenda for the year or the next couple of years and have the luxury of engaging in long, inefficient conversations—the kinds where genuinely new thinking has the chance to emerge. Attendees at a regular department meeting are always mindful of their next commitment that day. In a department retreat, in contrast, you've set aside a full workday outside the regular schedule and have agreed as a group to stretch out into it. As you can probably tell, I'm a big fan.

What topics are suited to a retreat? The following list is neither prescriptive nor exhaustive, of course, but might give an idea of the right size for agenda items:

- A discussion of leadership succession in the department (i.e., "Who chairs next?")
- Significant curricular reform—the writing of a new major or minor or significant revision of the current major or minor
- Hiring plans (or a hiring wish list) for the next two, three, and five years
- Discussing and beginning to draft a departmental self-study*
- Strategizing about how to promote the department, its courses, and its majors and/or minors among students
- Considering fund-raising needs/opportunities
- Planning a visiting speakers series

A department retreat is where urgent issues are put aside for a day so that faculty can remind themselves of why they do this work and what they want to see the department achieve in the next year or two. Depending on the focus of a given retreat, work with an outside facilitator can free up faculty members to entertain complex new proposals and can of course inject new thinking into departmental conversations.

One nice thing about a retreat, especially if you can secure a meeting place with sufficient space, is the opportunity to break out into some smaller groups for conversation. We know this can be effective, which is why we do it with our students, but the space and time constraints of regular department meetings don't really allow for it. Breaking up into groups of two, three, or four for a short period and having those groups report back to the full department can be a productive way of advancing the group's thinking on complex topics and allows everyone to speak.

---

*However, as a rule, tasks that are primarily writing assignments don't fare well in large group settings.

As is the case with regular department meetings, follow-through and follow-up will be key. If a retreat is held on a weekday, perhaps in the waning weeks of the summer, for instance, by the time classes are back in session and the first regular department meeting of the year rolls around, most faculty will have forgotten much of what was discussed and decided in the retreat. Minutes of the retreat need to be kept and circulated shortly after the retreat ends, and the action items and conclusions arrived at during the retreat need to feed into the academic-year discussions held by the department and be put into practice. In some cases, this will be facilitated by the creation of small ad hoc groups within the department. If the department has decided to create a minor, for instance, a few faculty might meet outside regular department meetings to research the structure of similar minors at peer institutions and/or the recommendations of professional organizations for the structure and content of the minor. Don't be afraid to let these groups assemble themselves; affinity regarding an issue or even personal affinity can help provide the energy to bring the task to completion.

After a successful retreat, just like after a successful department meeting, you'll feel like you've accomplished a lot. Most likely, though, you'll simply have committed to accomplishing a lot. The real work happens in between the meetings, and as chair, it's primarily your job to ensure that the follow-through happens.

Chapter 8

Dealing with Stress and Conflict

As I write this chapter about stress and intradepartmental and interpersonal conflict, I find myself immersed in an environment of stress and intradepartmental and interpersonal conflict.

But then, I could have written that sentence any time in the past 30 years (and that's not including graduate school, which was hardly stress free). Stress and conflict of various kinds aren't weird aberrations in the academic life. I don't make this observation flippantly; the truth is, they're the norm. As a faculty member at a college or university, you're working with very smart, very talented, very ambitious colleagues, the best at what they do. In 2018, under 2% of the US adult population had earned a PhD, and of those who undertake the degree with the hope of teaching at the college or university level, an increasingly small number are able to find permanent positions. However, the things that have made your colleagues successful in their professional endeavors can often be the same things that make collegiality difficult. We faculty tend to be a bit rough around the edges: we went to graduate school, not a finishing school, and what little finish there be we ordinarily (and rightly) reserve for our students. As chair it's your job, to the best of your ability, to hold this fragile ecosystem (or egosystem) together. And that's going to mean, among other things, learning to put your own ego on ice.

The Designated Grown-up

In his book *We Scholars: Changing the Culture of the University*, David Damrosch presents a cunning diagnosis (or perhaps etiology) of the situation. He lays the blame, in part, on the nature of our credentialing process: earning a PhD in the humanities, for instance, requires seven years (on average) of graduate study, most of which is undertaken in near solitude. As Damrosch delicately puts it, "The progressive isolation we enforce on graduate students favors personalities who have relatively little need for extended intellectual exchange."* In other words, we've created a process that favors faculty members who do their best work alone. We shouldn't, then, be surprised that such a process implicitly selects against those who thrive on interaction with others: rather, we should be amazed that anyone who needs such interaction ever makes it through. In the academy, to paraphrase Barbra Streisand, people who don't need people are the luckiest people in the world.†

I would hasten to add—although I haven't always appreciated this the way I do now—that this loose and variable commitment

---

*David Damrosch, *We Scholars: Changing the Culture of the University* (Cambridge: Harvard University Press, 1995), 9–10.

†The COVID-19 pandemic has thrown some of these issues into sharp relief. For a meditation on introvert scholars in the time of COVID, see Kevin Dettmar, "Garbo Was Wrong," *Inside Higher Ed*, March 25, 2021, https://www.insidehighered.com/advice/2021/03/25/professor-reflects-how-covid-has-taught-him-autonomy-differs-isolation-opinion.

to norms of collegiality is probably the inevitable price of doing the kind of business we do; it creates the conditions of freedom that are essential for creative work. As a result, one facet of the chair's job is a role I secretly call the designated grown-up. Let me explain what I mean.

Because I went straight from graduate school into a faculty position, I don't have much real experience with workplace teams and meetings outside colleges and universities. The things I've observed in academic workplaces may generalize to other kinds of work environments; I simply don't know. But here's something I've learned about department faculties: they do their work best when they know that someone in the room is taking responsibility for reporting out, reporting up, and taking ownership of the results. This dynamic allows faculty members to dream big, to pursue creative and untested ideas to their sometimes wildly impractical ends. It allows the id to run wild without bringing the superego to bear. And that's because—in this analogy—you, the department chair, are the superego and you recognize that it's most productive if you don't bring the hammer down too soon.

Playing this role is just about as much fun as it sounds. I've used the term designated grown-up, but you're also the designated wet blanket, the designated killjoy. I remember an instance of this that happened nearly a decade ago as if it were yesterday. We were in a department meeting, discussing a cost-cutting directive that had come down to departments from the dean's office. My colleagues weren't happy about it and were thinking "creatively," let's say, about some end runs. It was clear to me that some of them wouldn't pass muster with the administration: no, purchasing wine for a reception and pretending it's toner isn't going to fool anyone in the accounting office. But as the conversation ran its reckless course, we actually found ourselves in some very fruitful terrain. As a result, we created some partnerships with other departments to spread out the cost of our programming. This had the unanticipated bonuses of better participation and deeper ties to colleagues across the college. I know that for myself, it's a temptation to jump in during "pie in the sky" conversations and say, "The dean will never allow . . ." But if you can put that censor on hold for just a bit, you may just discover that such conversations turn up very creative and exciting suggestions (alongside some impractical ones).

The Use and Misuse of Collegiality

While we hold faculty members pretty strictly to account for treating their students with respect (through regular course evaluations and teaching observations, for instance), we have few such checks on collegiality. And collegiality, of course, can be an oppressive way to impose groupthink.

What, then, is to be done? The system of academic tenure provides strong safeguards of academic freedom, such that while faculty nominally inhabit an intermediate rung in a hierarchy (have a look at your institution's organizational chart), they look and act very much like free agents on a day-to-day basis. Strong institutional norms can enforce standards of professional behavior and collegiality until the awarding of tenure (at those institutions fortunate to have it). But once that ultimate reward has been won, no one—not colleagues, not a department chair or program director, not a dean, provost, president, or chancellor—really has very much leverage. An ancient adage says that with great power comes great responsibility, but in the academy, collegiality is not one of those responsibilities.

This puts chairs in a difficult position: they have the responsibility to foster a collegial working environment in the department (or at least the expectation from their colleagues and supervisors), but they have little authority to make that happen. The welfare of the department depends upon the goodwill of individual faculty members. So what are the sources of stress and conflict among a department's faculty? And what role can a department chair play in working to alleviate them?

1. Feeling Unappreciated

A former colleague once explained to me that most faculty grievances grow out of the source Satan identified in the opening lines of *Paradise Lost*; he tells Beëlzebub of his "high disdain, from sense of injur'd merit" (*PL* I.98). In choosing the academy over other professions, faculty members often believe themselves to have chosen prestige over earnings, so that prestige becomes the coin of the realm—and there's never quite enough to go around.

As chair, there are things you can do to address this situation, although they may not be enough. But at the very least, it will help if you agree that as chair you must be a tireless cheerleader for your faculty. We've all come through a credentialing system that rewards individual accomplishment, so this may feel a bit counterintuitive at first, but as chair, you must learn to celebrate vicariously through your colleague's achievements. Their triumphs are yours because you're creating the conditions that make it possible for them to thrive.

There are some simple ways to do this. Although they're not to everyone's taste, I'm a big fan of the handwritten note. I keep a box of notecards in my desk, and when an accomplishment of one of my colleagues comes to my attention, I send a short note of congratulations. Because faculty members are typically very competitive, there may not be much such recognition coming from their peers: let it come from you. It needn't be long, or overly detailed: the main message is simply, "I see you."

But don't let it stop there. An email to the department faculty letting everyone know that Prof. Armstrong has just won a prize from her national organization or that Prof. Patel has an article in the newest volume of the *Journal of Smarts* may irk some of your colleagues—in my experience, they'll appreciate your tooting your colleague's horn only slightly more than they would appreciate you tooting your own—but it will mean a great deal to those whose professional accomplishment might otherwise go unnoticed. Alternatively, or in addition, make it a point to mention these accomplishments during regularly scheduled department meetings under announcements or new business. And there's no reason to stop there: if your department has any kind of regular newsletter, make sure to notice it there, too, and make sure that your dean and/or provost and their staff are made aware and that the communications department gets the information for the college's web site or other promotional communication. Once your colleagues realize that you've taken this work on yourself, they'll be incredibly grateful. I'm no psychologist, but I'm persuaded that those who annoyingly toot their own horns do so only out of fear that if they don't do it, no one will. Be the horn tooter.

One caution: if you commit to this assignment, you've got to be ecumenical. You've got to celebrate the work both of the colleagues you admire and those you quietly dislike and you've got to recognize work that you find important and work in which you have little interest. In order to ensure equal and fair coverage, tell your colleagues in no uncertain terms that you want them to inform you of their accomplishments: make it safe, to continue with this tired metaphor, for them to toot their horns to you privately. You'll want to set professional minima, depending on the research expectations of your discipline, department, or institution. For instance, will I share conference presentations or only published work? Work accepted for publication or only work in print? Invited pieces or only peer-reviewed research and juried creative work? And so on. There are no right answers to these questions, but I know from painful experience that if you plan to announce publications and a colleague excitedly sends you word of an acceptance, they'll be hurt if that news fails to clear a bar that you haven't made explicit.

2. Emotional Reactivity

As David Damrosch muses in the passage quoted above, it seems likely that our profession has unconsciously biased itself toward members with a particular emotional makeup. As he puts it in one of the book's blunter passages, "We have built up a system that gives high marks to people who flunk sandbox."* At my graduate institution, legend preserves the moment when a member of the faculty stood up during a faculty meeting and said the unspeakable: "Let's just admit it: we were all the kids that none of the other kids wanted to play with." I remember a friend who was the graduate student representative in that meeting emerging from the room, horrified. It was if he'd seen a ghost (the Ghost of Career Future). I'm painting with a broad brush here while hoping not to descend into caricature; certainly *I* wasn't one of those kids, and probably you weren't either. But as a faculty member, and especially as a chair, you're going to be dealing with some folks who have a less fully formed interpersonal skill set than some of their nonacademic peers.

I have a corollary to Damrosch's law, and it applies to you, dear reader. If Damrosch's law is something like "Academic training leads to a club of the unclubbable," then Dettmar's corollary is "And those who *are* clubable yet make it through academic training are destined to be chairs, directors, deans, provosts, and presidents."

How can a chair successfully negotiate these complicated affective waters? There's no easy answer, but one piece of advice might help if you're able to follow it (and it's not easy). Recognize that your relationships with your colleagues are not friendships; they are collegial working relationships, even when those colleagues are your friends—perhaps *especially* when those colleagues are your friends. Don't expect your interactions with colleagues to be reciprocally generous and supportive. That's not what they're meant to be. They're intended to be largely unidirectional: you're in your role in order to support your colleagues, not to be supported by them.

This can be very fraught when you are friends with some, even many, of the colleagues you now serve as their chair. No one

*Damrosch, *We Scholars*, 10.

would suggest that you need to sever or even change the terms of those friendships now that you're chair: chairs need friends too! But you must effect a conscious separation of those roles and understand that when you're relating to a colleague as a friend, they may understand the exchange differently. You'll be well served to erect as good a firewall between those roles as you're able.

One compensation I've found is that as chair, I have a new cohort of colleagues: other department chairs and program directors. In this case, it's role rather than discipline that binds us, but that's a lot. They will understand the challenges, both bureaucratic and emotional, of your position; they will have experiences and advice to share. While you are not leaving your department peers behind, during your time as chair you gain an additional set of professional mentors and friends. Their counsel and just their informed listening will help you contend with issues you cannot bring to your department colleagues.

3. Philosophical/Ideological Differences

There's a famous saying attributed variously to Henry Kissinger or Wallace Stanley Sayre that "academic politics are so vicious precisely because the stakes are so small." It's not a fair characterization unless you accept its underlying premise that ideas don't really matter. But it's certainly accurate when it comes to the intensity of some faculty disagreements.

In my experience, these ideological positions aren't thrown on and off like an old T-shirt: they're not mere postures, faddish position-taking. They are most often deeply held and connected to deep-seated belief systems and ways of understanding how the world works. Which suggests that the way forward when faculty clash over these positions lies not in trying to stifle them but instead in appealing to colleagues' commitment to larger frameworks that all faculty members embrace: to supporting our students in their learning and to the free inquiry that is a pillar of academic freedom and that the tenure system is meant to guarantee. Because

I value academic freedom, I concede my economics department colleague's right to make supply-side arguments and publish in conservative journals and even to teach supply-side theory, even though my own orientation suggests that they're on the wrong path. And because I'm committed to my students' flourishing and believe that students are best served when they encounter a diversity of viewpoints in their education, I'm committed to creating a space where we can each teach from our own perspectives, from our own expertise.

To be sure, an appeal to the welfare of your students can backfire: colleagues can argue that certain ideologies are dangerous or that the contest of ideas within a department or curriculum presents a distraction to students. And it is sometimes the case that students are used as symbolic shields to fend off positions we find objectionable. But unless yours is a narrowly focused curriculum that all department faculty have agreed to support, your job is chair is to make sure that a vibrant ideological/philosophical/theoretical diversity flourishes in the work of your faculty and finds appropriate expression in your curricula and course offerings.

4. Changing Chair Styles

This might sound like a bit out of a novel—actually, it *is* a bit out of a novel. I assumed my first chair's job as the result of a department's national search and moved 500 miles to a new university to take over the job. I didn't know a lot about the department's history. It perhaps comes as no surprise that departments with a fractious past do their best to cover up that history when recruiting a new faculty member, never mind a new chair. In the process of moving, I sustained an injury for which I required minor surgery and a friend, a professor at another university, sent me a care package containing, among other items, a copy of Richard Russo's academic satire, *Straight Man*.

My friend meant well. It's a ripping good yarn, and I was thoroughly enjoying it and thoroughly forgetting my pain—until I gradually realized that the school that was being satirized was the school I had just moved to. The department being mocked was my new department; the novel's protagonist, a department chair—a charming, albeit tough-talking old-school rainmaker—was the guy whose resignation had created the opening I had filled.

My amusement turned to horror, of course; and to be fair, my friend had no idea that my department was the model for the novel (although Russo had taught there for a good spell). What was so upsetting for me about *Straight Man* wasn't the plot—any academic is used to campus satires, and a writer who would mockingly name a character He/She to ridicule their efforts at gender inclusivity inhabits a pretty different part of the academy from me. No, what was upsetting was to learn, in the pages of a novel, about the Mafia-style management techniques of my predecessor—someone who had enjoyed a good deal of success during his long tenure and whose methods I think many of my new colleagues expected me to adopt. (In the novel, the English department chair threatens to kill one goose in the campus lake every day until his budget is approved by the dean. Fortunately, I never had the sense that I was expected to do that.)

Although I never saw the real-life model in action as chair, I certainly bore little resemblance to the man who inspired that character in *Straight Man*, and although I distanced myself from many of his strategies, there was no question but that he was effective in securing resources for the department. Thus, much of the criticism that I got from my new colleagues during our early days together was based (probably subconsciously) on the kind of pattern my predecessor had established. Perhaps nothing but the passing of time will help in such a situation. As your tenure as chair expands and your faculty colleagues see that you're committed to the department's and their own well-being and that there's more than one way to lead a department, you'll become the model by which they subconsciously measure the success of your successor.

5. Generational Shifts

Some of this area of tension is captured in the discussion of ideological and philosophical differences above: different theoreti-
cal models have dominated the thought of different eras in our
fields of study. These models influenced our graduate training
and often our early years as faculty members. For this reason
alone, two faculty members in a department separated in age by
25 or 30 years may have profoundly different orientations to their
work.

But the differences aren't limited to methodology and theory:
they find expression, too, in our understanding of what consti-
tutes good teaching and what a rewarding professional career
consists of. In my own field, I was first hired into a tenure-track
position in a department that wouldn't have interviewed any applicants who hadn't already published in scholarly journals. But at
the same time, it had senior faculty members who hadn't published much more than an article or two in careers spanning decades. It's not, of course, that the newer generation of scholars
were better, more accomplished, more savvy: it's that they were
trained, and culled, according to more aggressive "publish or per-
ish" standards that eventually made their way from elite research
universities to smaller, teaching-oriented institutions. When I was
interviewing for entry-level jobs three decades ago, my credentials
were being scrutinized by faculty members whose research, at
least, didn't compare with mine, and three decades later I find the
I am evaluating candidates whose research is judged by different
standards than mine was when I first went on the market.

While it would be a mistake to codify this too minutely, surely
it makes some sense to respect the expectations, the professional
and institutional norms, under which colleagues came into their
current positions instead of engaging in cross-generational war-
fare. Just as the relative weights of teaching, research, and service
tend to vary across a faculty member's career, so too do they dif-

fer from one generation of scholars to the next, and academic work should be evaluated in the proper context. In my field, Wayne Booth's *The Rhetoric of Fiction*, which has been called "the single most important American contribution to narrative theory,"* was published in 1961. It was the first book of an illustrious career. Booth finished his PhD in 1950; the book took a decade to complete. Under today's conditions, it's a book that likely would never have been published and its author would never have earned tenure.

6. Communication: How Is Information Disseminated?

We touched on this before, but it bears repeating here: one-on-one communication is invaluable but unreliable. When you're the chair and you're hearing the perspective of just one colleague in communication between just the two of you, you're vulnerable to being influenced by what the colleague is saying, whether or not that is their intention. Just as bad, when other colleagues learn that you've been communicating this way in one-on-one meetings, they'll quickly become suspicious that some members of the department have more direct access to the chair's authority than others.

For these and other reasons, in-person and one-on-one communications must be balanced by regular, inclusive, written communications about information that's important to all members of the department and by regular meetings of the department faculty. If you're using email to convey information to the entire department, pay attention to all the normal guidelines for formal business communication: keep your emails as brief (and as infrequent) as possible, craft informative subject lines, read and reread

*Mary Rourke, "Wayne Booth, 84; Teacher of Literary Criticism, Wrote 'The Rhetoric of Fiction,'" *Los Angeles Times*, October 14, 2005, https://www.latimes.com/archives/la-xpm-2005-oct-14-me-booth14-story.html.

and reread your text before hitting send, and be careful about the cc's and bcc's. And make sure that if your message alludes to an attachment, you remember to attach it!

When you are a department chair, there is a chance that some people will read your social media accounts differently. Even though you may think of these channels as personal, any professional connections who are in your network may read your posts and pics as coming ex cathedra. In addition, because you have become part of The Institution in the eyes of some colleagues, your posts may be read as part of a coordinated institutional communications strategy and may come in for criticism directed at the institution. Some faculty members create separate personal accounts and restrict their personal postings to them. When a junior colleague was coming up for tenure, they wrote me to say that they were going to unfriend me, their chair, on Facebook, not because we'd stopped being friendly but because the confusion of the personal and professional had started to seem too risky. It seemed like a sensible move to me.

Handling Conflict with the Faculty You Lead

Up to this point, I've been focusing on conflict among your faculty colleagues. If only that were the worst of it. But of course, since you're nominally first among equals in your department and are perceived to have some degree of institutional power (which is perhaps more symbolic than real), you're not just going to be refereeing conflicts. You'll be a participant in at least some of them.

For six intense months, my wife and I had the distinction of having four teenagers under our roof. It was the best of times, it was the worst of times. I came up with an aphorism that became something of a mantra for us that we'd repeat when things got tough, something I cobbled together out of a rudimentary understanding of Freud and structuralism: "It's not personal; it's structural." Which is to say, as we literary critics would put it, some of our interactions with our children were overdetermined: sometimes, larger structures than our own particular experiences shaped the lines both sides were reciting.

That's true, too, of a chair's relationship with some of their faculty colleagues. When a person moves from faculty member to chair, they surrender their humanity, at least in the eyes of some of their colleagues. For a smart bunch, we can be pretty stupid about this: we're comfortable talking about "faculty" and "administration" in starkly Manichean terms, as if the two circles in that Venn diagram don't overlap. Depending on the size and structure of your institution, your positionality as chair can be somewhat ambiguous. The institution where I first served as chair had a unionized faculty. This made the lines between faculty and administration all the more rigid owing to a history of mistrust on both sides (a structural mistrust). When I came into the department and the university, I thought of myself as a faculty colleague, albeit one who was responsible for supporting the work of the department faculty; I was a faculty member who was temporarily assigned to chair the department. The faculty weren't so sure; under the union rules, department chairs weren't part of the bargaining unit. By the terms of the faculty contract, we weren't members of the faculty. (I quickly realized that voluntarily paying monthly union dues was an important gesture of solidarity, even though the union was not bargaining on my behalf.) Meanwhile, there was never any question in the minds of senior administration that mine was a faculty appointment rather than an administrative one. In effect, the faculty said, "not one of us," and the administration said the same. The situation called to mind the Edward Everett Hale story "The Man without a Country"—or more ominously, the Magazine song "Shot by Both Sides." A target on both my chest and on my back.

That's an extreme case, to be sure, but the fact is that once you take on the chair's role in your department, whether as a longtime member or an outside hire, you'll be "othered," to some extent, by some or many of the members of your department. And part of the otherness of your role is that you're in a position to exert at least some authority and you have the power to exert at least some influence over the work lives of your colleagues. In many systems, for instance, the chair makes a direct report to the dean about annual faculty performance and sometimes about merit calculations that factor into salary increases. When you have a role to play in someone's pay in a system where there are winners and losers, you will pay for that influence. For this reason, in part, many systems legislate an independent merit review committee whose recommendations can be more or less binding on the chair. But in my experience, even when working with such a committee, I was the one who was thanked when a healthy raise came through—and the one blamed when no increase was forthcoming. (I was delighted to learn, when coming to my current institution, that chairs have no role in annual faculty evaluations or salary adjustments. I've never known what any of my colleagues make, and in this case, at least, ignorance is bliss.)

In a similar dynamic, but with more dire outcomes, most tenure and promotion procedures put department chairs in a pivotal role. In nearly all institutions, the chair is responsible for overseeing (and often for writing) the department's review of tenure and promotion candidates and other forms of faculty contract renewal. For obvious reasons, this can be some of the most sensitive and fraught work a chair is called upon to do and (along with hiring) the most consequential. It can also prove one of (if not the most) important source of conflict in a department between faculty colleagues or between faculty and the chair.

About Herding Those Cats . . .

So faculty colleagues can be difficult. News flash: human relationships are difficult. In-laws are difficult, friends are difficult, parents are difficult, children are difficult. Are collegial faculty relationships more difficult than these others? Well, certainly they have that reputation: the hoary metaphor is that chairing a department is like herding cats. But I'd like to close this chapter by reprinting a thoughtful Facebook post that Caren Irr, then chair of the English department at Brandeis University, wrote on August 25, 2019. It brings some real and necessary nuance to that cartoonish oversimplification.

Preparing for what I expect to be my last year as chair of my department and reflecting on that cliché about managing academics being like herding cats. Here's what I know about cats:

1. You don't herd them because a lot of them don't like to be too close to other cats.
2. A cat is more likely to come over to you if you entice it with a tasty treat it hasn't enjoyed in a while.
3. Cats are not really that into the toys that you can buy in a store, but they will often make their own toys out of stuff lying around the house. Use those.
4. Once you have a cat's attention, you typically have to keep petting it if you don't want to get scratched.
5. The scratches are not really that bad but they do take a while to heal.
6. If a cat hisses, it is because it feels backed into a corner or perceives another creature as being too close to its territory. Give it some space.
7. Sometimes you don't see a happy cat for quite a while.
8. At the same time, cats do get mad when you go away for too long.
9. A cat that is making noises is usually not sick; just trying to get some attention.
10. All cats have dignity and elegant form, even those that give you the stink eye.

Take good care of the cats entrusted to your care.

Chapter 9

Connecting the Department to the School, College, and/or University

In the modern American university, it is possible (even common) for faculty members to have very little engagement with the institution above the level of their home department. If a college or university is like a house, the department is the living room or bedroom: a comfortable (one hopes) home within the home. But of course departments have connections and responsibilities to the institution they are situated in, even if many faculty members relish their niche in the department and largely ignore the bigger picture in order to focus their attention and energies on their students and their research. In this chapter, I direct my gaze outside the department to its role in the larger ecosystem of the school, college, and/or university and to its relationship (and yours, as the department's representative) to the dean and/or the provost. If departments often exhibit isolationist tendencies, a kind of inward, centripetal propensity, part of your job as chair is to ensure that your unit and your faculty colleagues stay healthily connected to the larger mission of your institution. You don't want your faculty to ignore your institution, and most certainly you don't want your institution to ignore your department.

Preparing the Ground for Resource Requests

Despite the promise of a slogan like "every tub on its own bottom" (Harvard's description, taken from John Bunyan's *Pilgrim's Progress*, of its system in which every school within the university supports itself), a better motto for the academic department might be a paraphrase of John Donne: "No department is an island, entire of itself." A department can appear to operate with relative autonomy only if there's a department chair who realizes that such autonomy is something of an illusion and who takes upon themself the vital work of maintaining the department's relationship to the other units and the administrative structure of the campus. That is to say, as chair you worry about the institutional ecosystem and your department's place in it so that, for the most part, your faculty colleagues don't have to.

Your department doesn't possess the means to support its own operations. At the very least, the salaries of your faculty and staff, and at most, nearly all of your costs are borne centrally by the institution. In order for those resources to continue to flow to your department, you will need to ensure that certain mandatory forms of reporting are attended to. You'll also want to be on the lookout for other opportunities to share the story of the good work your faculty colleagues are doing, for it's only when that good work becomes known and recognized that you can reasonably ask for additional resources to support it.

It might seem obvious that your dean or provost would be aware of the work being done by your department faculty, but in my experience, this is a dangerous thing to take for granted. A couple of years into one of my appointments as chair, I realized that my department had a somewhat mixed reputation in the dean's office, owing largely to incidents and personalities that predated my arrival at the institution. We were perceived as low performing, whereas in truth our faculty were publishing research and creative work at a very healthy clip. We decided to attack this reputational problem indirectly and in a way that would be enjoyable for all involved: we started to host small gatherings in the department whenever a faculty member published a new book. This was a great way to shine a light on a faculty member who may have been laboring in near isolation on a project for years, and it felt important to celebrate these accomplishments for our students, to give them insight into the work and time frames of scholarship. But secretly, the college administration was an important, if unacknowledged, audience for these events: we wanted a way to make our administrators aware of the good work that was being done in the department. Everyone from faculty colleagues in other departments through the dean and up to the president was invited to these book-launch parties.

Of course, it shouldn't fall entirely to you, the department chair, or to your colleagues to make visible the work you're doing in the department: that's why most colleges and universities have communications departments.* It's the job of the communications staff at your institution to get the story of your department out to students, potential students and their families, alumni, outside media, and potential donors. Since one particularly rewarding aspect of the chair's work is shining a light on the accomplishments of faculty colleagues, this collaboration should be a welcome one. One of the benefits of making sure that your communications team knows of the achievements of your faculty is that they will put these achievements onto the radar of your senior administrators. Although it can feel like you're pestering the communications team when you pass news along to them, in fact they're always grateful for items that they can put out to their various audiences. And if you as chair make sure to

---

*I mean here communications that would be part of your institution's administration (handling public affairs, media requests, the institution's website), not the academic department of communications.

communicate the accomplishments of your faculty colleagues instead of expecting them to do so themselves, there's no boasting involved—or at most, it will be the forgivable boasting of a proud colleague. Just as long as you're not making a mountain out of a molehill (trying to secure landing-page placement on the university's web site for a faculty colleague's presentation to a community group, for example), the staff of your communications unit will be grateful for your leads.

Preparing for Program Review

Although we're all naturally anxious at the prospect of outside evaluation of our work, many of us have probably also had the experience that such review can be a real tonic if we go into it prepared, are able to present our work in the best light, and earnestly seek strategies for making it better. Most colleges and universities undertake regular self-study and outside program-review exercises, often on a 10-year cycle—which means that a chair serving a three-year term stands a good chance of needing to oversee the research and writing of the self-study, the visit by the review team, and/or the response to the outside reviewers' report, the department's equivalent of the institution's accreditation review. Faculty members often view these reviews, like the larger institutional reviews, with skepticism: they require a huge investment of time, and in some institutional settings, few if any resources are available to address the suggestions for improvement the review team makes. But the most salient insights contained in the outside reviewers' report will be quoted and requoted for years in documents circulating at your institution, and while writing the self-study report and hosting the outside review team are both jobs for the full faculty, as department chair the burden will land on you to make sure the exercise provides as much value for your colleagues as possible.

The department's self-study is a long, research-intensive, and rather formal piece of writing. As the time approaches for its preparation, you will receive instruction from, and perhaps have a meeting with, your dean or provost. One of the first questions (whether or not you're invited to engage with your dean or provost about it) is who ought to be asked to serve on the outside review team. These teams are usually composed of two or three scholars from other institutions. At least one of them should be from a peer institution, a college or university with a similar mission and ethos to your own. You will be in a better position than your dean to know which scholars of your discipline would be best suited to evaluate your department. It's important, to the degree possible in a small team, to represent the various areas of expertise of your department among the reviewers.

Although your dean or provost is under no obligation to accept your suggestions—they're paying for the review and it's you and your colleagues (and your program) that are being reviewed—it would be a very unusual situation (and a very bad sign) if the dean were to ignore your advice completely. In conversation with your colleagues, you should think about both the level and type of expertise of the outside reviewers you recommend. Close professional friends might provide reassurance, but ideally you want reviewers who will ask difficult questions, bring their experience of working in a high-performing department to bear, and provide a review that is tough, fair, and constructive. If you choose just close colleagues, you might have a path to sweeping your department's problems under the rug, but if you do, the process will be just as demanding and time consuming as it would be if you chose a more rigorous team of reviewers and at the end you won't have very much to show for it.

The self-study document the department prepares will have to conform quite closely to guidelines your dean or provost provides. In addition to whatever guidance and/or template they might provide, you'd be well advised to also look at some self-study documents generated at your institution—your own department's most recent self-study (and the resulting outside reviewers' report) at least, but ideally also a recent self-study from a cognate unit on your campus. Although as chair you will oversee the preparation and submission of the self-study document, it's too much to take on alone. This is the quintessential example of writing by committee. At a series of department meetings or, ideally, an all-day retreat, your department faculty will have to divide up responsibility for various sections of the document. Your responsibility, unless you're able to delegate this and are comfortable with doing so, will be to pull the disparate pieces by different hands into one coherent document. Make sure to look at the requirements for the self-study as soon as you have them. Some pieces, such as data from the registrar, the alumni office, and other campus units, will take some time to acquire, and you'll need to put in those requests right away.

When your dean or provost has assembled the review team and your department's self-study is in the team members' hands, a campus visit will be scheduled to enable the reviewers to examine the material conditions of your work; interview students, faculty, and staff; and follow up with department faculty and the institution's administration regarding further information they need, questions that remain, or clarification of claims made in the self-study.* During their time on campus, your role as department chair parallels in some ways the work involved in hosting job candidates: you coordinate hospitality and access to any documents or data the team might require and provide a convenient space where they can do their work without interruption. The outside review team usually completes its report within a month of the campus visit and submits it to the dean or provost, who will then forward a copy to you.

---

*Typically a review team will be on campus for two or three days. The provost's or dean's office pays for their services. Rates of compensation vary, but something in the range of $1,000-$2,000 is common. The honorarium is meant to recognize the time spent reading the self-study in preparation for the visit, the time on campus, and the work of putting together the team's report. The provost or the dean also covers the cost of reviewers' travel, accommodations, and meals.

The arrival of the report may occasion a meeting with your dean or provost to review and discuss its findings and recommendations. You should also schedule a meeting of department faculty to discuss the report before meeting with the administrator who commissioned it to ensure that you represent the sentiment(s) of the full department. When you receive such a document, you hope for a combination of broad praise and suggestions for making your department even better. Those recommendations for strengthening the department will become evidence in your requests for various kinds of resources over the coming years.

Advocating for Departmental Resources

In chapter 2, I discussed the need for and some strategies for requesting new faculty lines for hiring. A similar logic underlies other personnel requests, such as for staff positions, that you might make of your dean or provost. They must be well supported with documentation (course enrollments, FTEs,* your department's public programming and attendance figures, annual budget, and the outside reviewers' report) and reflect your awareness of the institution's strategic goals and the circumstances under which other departments (including departments like yours at peer institutions) do their work. Campus-wide staffing, like faculty hiring, is normally a zero-sum game: you're not arguing just for an additional administrative assistant in your department but also implicitly arguing that you should have the position instead of the psychology department. Under normal circumstances, the pie's not getting any bigger; you're fighting for a bigger piece of what's already there.

The same holds true for other kinds of budgetary requests. Ordinarily, institutions have an annual calendar and funding requests from departments are due once a year. For requests that

*Full-time equivalents, an aggregation of the full- and part-time teaching faculty in your department.

grow out of your department's long-term planning, this is the right time to make your needs known. At some institutions there is another, albeit sometimes informal, moment near the end of the fiscal year when some unspent monies will disappear if not used. This is when a dean or provost may entertain additional funding requests. It's not a bad idea at such institutions to keep a list with your department's desiderata at a range of costs, making it possible for you to submit requests for last-minute funding opportunities such as these.

At most institutions, departments are housed within a particular campus building. In some systems, a chair will have the opportunity to assign office and laboratory space to faculty in their building—in consultation with other chairs, if the building is shared with other departments or programs. At some institutions, though, space assignments, like faculty positions, are controlled centrally. A chair in such a system will normally be involved in consulting about and facilitating the office assignments without actually making them. Beyond its practical import, of course, campus space carries tremendous symbolic weight: a large and light-filled office is not just more pleasant to work in, it also signals to others that the institution values its occupant. Your department will have a system in place for assigning spaces and/or for offering newly vacated spaces to faculty (for instance, by rank or by seniority). Your faculty will interpret any perceived breach in those protocols as a sign of favor or disfavor. Step carefully. Follow the guidelines. Be transparent.

The Chair as Liaison between Department and Institution

The chair's role in articulating the department's needs and accomplishments to the administration and in conveying the administration's expectations back to the department can be an exhausting one. In its most extreme form, we're looking at a Venn diagram like the one I invoked earlier. In this one, the circle labeled

"Department" and the circle labeled "College" or "University" overlap only slightly and you, department chair, are that area of intersection. It's also your responsibility to keep your department's faculty and staff colleagues apprised of university news, especially updates that you may receive in the chairs' meetings your dean convenes, and to keep university administrators up to date on the news in your department. These two communications roles are asymmetrical in a number of ways. For one, administrators will often ask you to be the bearer of bad news to your faculty; when there's good news, they're happy to bring it themselves (and get the credit). A president or provost will write to faculty to announce raises; you, on the other hand, will probably be tasked with bringing the news of a budget cut to your faculty. By the same token, a wise chair will not wear out the path to their dean's office to discuss every concern or complaint that arises in the course of their work. Be especially leery of exhausting the goodwill of your dean by asking for meetings simply so you can tell your faculty colleagues that you have done so. To be sure, sometimes a decision that needs to be made is above your pay grade; when you don't have the authority to act on something that needs to be done, it's time to confer with your dean. But over time, a dean or provost will appreciate it (even if only subconsciously) if you come to them only when it's absolutely necessary to do so. They'll be more willing to meet with you and work with you if they recognize you as a chair who genuinely respects their time.

So by the tacit agreement of both your faculty colleagues and the administrators you report to, you are both the liaison between your department's faculty and the administration and between the administration and the faculty. In such a position, there's a strong temptation to mischaracterize either party to the other—to present the request of a faculty member to your dean with a roll of your eyes or bring a directive from the dean back to the department accompanied by a "just between us" running commentary for the benefit of your colleagues. (This is perhaps a logical result of the chair's status as not fully faculty and not fully administration.) Just don't do it: it's corrosive, and it promulgates a facile kind of caricature that needs to be avoided, a stark binarism that pits faculty against administrators in a simplistic way. With some exceptions at the very highest administrative levels of some institutions, the administration—the head of academic affairs, for instance, whether it is a dean or a provost—was trained as a scholar or creator and teacher and came up through the academic ranks. As department chair, you're liable to be tarred with this same kind of rhetoric (i.e., that you've "gone over to the dark side": see above). As comforting as it is to rage against the machine, the fact is that you need to do both sides of your job— the administration-facing side and the faculty-facing side—with integrity.

By the same token, it's your responsibility to represent the concerns of your faculty to your dean with integrity, assuming that you share those concerns or at least consider them to be valid. You need to act as an honest broker, even when it's tempting to downplay a colleague's issue in a misguided attempt to curry favor with the administration. It's an unalterable existential truth of the chair's role that you're neither fully faculty nor fully administration, and no amount of gamesmanship or double dealing is going to spare you the difficulties that creates. The only solution is to be a person of integrity, respected by both sides as a trustworthy representative of the needs and concerns of faculty and the priorities of administration.

Besides the dean's office, you'll want to attend to many other working relationships that are important to the flourishing of your department. Keeping cordial relationships with the registrar's office, the room scheduler's office, the communications team, the finance office, and the advancement office, among others, will ensure that your requests for various kinds of support services receive timely attention.

Whose Side Are You On?

Early during my first stint chairing a department, I was waylaid after a department tenure meeting by the director of graduate studies. In my memory, they pinned me to the wall in the hallway, although that can't be right. But I do remember what they said: I'd just voted with a small minority of the department faculty against tenure for a colleague, someone the graduate director was closer to than I was and had worked longer with than I had. Although tenure votes in this department were secret, I've always made it a policy of declaring my vote; such an important decision requires, in my mind at least, that I be accountable for it. In the case in question, the faculty member had very clearly not met the research requirements as set out by the department, the college, and the university: it wasn't even close. But the department faculty, for what I believe were charitable reasons, voted to support them anyway.

So the graduate director stopped me on my way back to my office and asked rather menacingly, "Whose side are you on? It's not just me—people in the department want to know. Are you with the department, or against us?" I thought it was a bizarre question. I'd recently uprooted my family and moved halfway across the country to chair this department. My wife had been forced to decline admission to the graduate program she'd been admitted to because of the move, and my oldest daughter had to spend her senior year in a new high school. We'd turned our lives upside down for this department and now my loyalty was being questioned.

On personal and professional grounds, I felt I could not support the case: tenure is awarded for meeting departmental and institutional criteria for teaching, research, and service, and in this case one of those marks had clearly not been met. The graduate director's question was based on a fundamental misunderstanding of the nature of the department's relationship to the college and the university. My being "with" the department couldn't simply mean co-signing on everything the department wanted to do. To me, it meant operating in good faith in the long-term strategic interests of the department. In the tenure case in question, there was no doubt in my mind (as subsequently proved to be true) that tenure would be denied at the college and university levels. Not only would our support not win tenure for our colleague, I also feared that the department would be perceived as not operating in good faith and that future personnel decisions would be viewed with suspicion. (This also proved to be the case, and institutions, administrators, and personnel committees can have surprisingly long memories.) This was at the institution I've mentioned previously with a unionized faculty, where both "faculty" and "administration" were reduced to cartoonish versions of the real thing—faculty in white hats, deans and provosts in black.

I worked for a short time under a department chair who liked to lean on just this kind of good cop/bad cop narrative when bringing news to the department from the chairs' meetings the dean convened. To hear them tell it, it was a David-and-Goliath-type situation—the powerful and inhuman dean announcing drastic measures that our valiant chair heroically opposed on our behalf (though seemingly without effect). Very quickly, though, the bad faith of this strategy became apparent to all of us: we knew that the dean was not the ogre they were being painted to be and that our chair wasn't really sticking their neck out on our behalf. Instead, they were seeking to burnish their own status with us through improbable stories of their selfless advocacy, and it wasn't a great leap to imagine them portraying us in equally cartoonish fashion when they met with the dean. Tempting though it sometimes is, your colleagues won't admire you for bad-mouthing the administration—and further, and perhaps worse, they won't believe you.

Indeed, in one working relationship with a dean that was unusually cordial, I was the beneficiary of a very different version of the good cop/bad cop routine. Although a chair's real authority varies depending on the institution, in very few systems, I would argue, does the chair really have the power to make some of the changes that they know would move the department forward. But in one situation, I worked with a dean who shared my vision for the department, at least in some of its aspects (they had served as chair of an English department themselves previously), and they were willing to take the heat for some decisions that needed to be made. That is to say, they were willing to play bad cop—to take responsibility for decisions I would have liked to make on my own but didn't quite have the authority to do so. I had an understanding with the dean that sometimes they were willing to use the authority at their disposal to help a thoughtful chair accomplish the things they hoped to in the department. We weren't working in opposition to one another but in harmony, and it was great. (Sadly, I've rarely experienced such teamwork since.)

Creating Peer Networks on Campus

Your dean will probably convene regular meetings of their department chairs and program directors (though I've worked with some who did not). These gatherings, and the list of other recipients in the emails announcing them, can help you connect with chairs of other units on campus for the purpose of peer advising. If your dean does not convene their department chairs, consider doing so yourself, and even if they do, an occasional separate, chairs-only gathering can be of great practical help, since some of what you'll want to confer with other chairs about is precisely how best to work with the dean. A chairs' meeting convened by the dean and one convened by (and of) department chairs are two very different kinds of meetings. I was always happiest when I had access to both.

The peer network of department chairs that I'm suggesting you foster will enable you to solicit advice and institutional wisdom that will help you perform your job better, but there are also many advantages to working with other departments on projects of mutual interest. In some cases, informal gatherings of department chairs for the purpose of sharing information and advice will help you in both respects.

But you should not be the only faculty member in your department who is connecting it to the larger institution. That's too much for you to carry: it's not sustainable and it's not healthy. Encourage some of your faculty colleagues to serve outside the department at the school, college, or university level. Consider nominating your faculty colleagues (with their permission) to key campus committees. They'll bring a broader perspective back to the department and you won't be only one to bring news to the department about the administration's plans at the college or university level. At department meetings you can make time on the agenda for them to report on news from their committees, which will help the department faculty better understand the work those committees do within the institution. At the same time, they'll be taking news from the department to the larger campus community they interact with, amplifying the work you're doing as chair to keep the work of the department on the radar of the administration.

As chair of your department, one essential function you can provide for your colleagues is to keep your eye on the big picture so that most of the time they can keep their focus on their classes, their students, and their research or creative activities. You will have access to information that they won't otherwise encounter or you will learn of it earlier, and you must endeavor to operate with integrity, carrying out your role as an honest broker in the two-way information flow between your department and the upper administration. And although no one else in your department will carry the weight of this in the way that you do, having colleagues who also engage with the institution above the level of the department can help validate the messages you bring from the administration and help you communicate the successes and needs of your department's colleagues to your dean and/or provost.

Chapter 10

Maintaining a Scholarly
or Creative Profile

One of the biggest objections that faculty members have to taking on the chair's role is the perception that their research or creative work will suffer. Most department chairs receive some kind of released time for their service, but few find, in practice, that the lighter teaching load makes up for the additional administrative responsibilities. To say it another way: only a fool would accept the chair's job for the course release. There may be exceptions, but for most of us, serving as chair makes it more difficult to advance our own work. Difficult, but not impossible. Since professors often view an assignment to chair as a mandated three-year drought in their own scholarly or creative output, in this chapter I'll explore strategies for keeping your professional activity alive during your term.*

---

*An earlier version of this chapter, cowritten with Laurie McMillen with the catalyst of an Association of Departments of English seminar, originally appeared in *ADE Bulletin* 154 (2015): 72-76.

Why Maintain a Research Profile?

Let's start with first principles. Unless you're still on the tenure clock at an institution with high research expectations, you may feel that you can afford a stint of lower-than-average productivity. Given all the demands on a chair's time and attention, why even try to keep your research moving forward? Not all chairs need or want to continue their scholarly work, so these remarks are not meant to be prescriptive.

However, a 1992 study found that 78.11% of chairs surveyed believe it is important to "remain current within [the] academic discipline." Additional priorities include "maintain[ing] research program and associated professional activities" (70.45%) and "obtain[ing] resources for personal research" (54.18%).* Thirty years later, it seems likely that scholarly work has become an even higher priority for reasons ranging from the personal to the professional. Perhaps the most compelling reason to continue with your scholarship is that your research interests and expertise are what led you to an academic department in the first place.

Attending to your research passions can have positive results beyond your own gratification. For one, scholarly accomplishment helps us maintain status and credibility with administrators, allowing us to advocate more effectively for our departments. At my institution, for instance, department chairs have an important voice in advocating for the tenure and promotion cases of their faculty colleagues. That voice carries more authority when the speaker has earned their colleagues' respect as a scholar or artist. Similarly, continuing scholarly work helps us serve as role models and mentors who can empathize with colleagues struggling to meet their research goals. Furthermore, research can inform and

*James B. Carroll and Walter H. Gmelch, "The Relationship of Department Chair Roles to Importance of Chair Duties" (paper presented at the annual meeting of the Association for the Study of Higher Education Annual Meeting, Minneapolis, MN, October 29, 1992), 5, https://archive.org/details/ERIC_ED352910.

revitalize our teaching and may open up opportunities for collaborative work with students. We may also benefit from staying active in the field as we embark on curricular reform, undertake program development, recruit faculty colleagues, or become involved in other administrative projects. In short, maintaining a research profile should be viewed as contributing to rather than competing with our administrative and teaching responsibilities.

In a larger sense, it's important that the culture of higher education administrative work become associated with growth and leadership, not with sacrifice. Chairs who subsequently move to a new institution or to a dean's position will benefit from a consistent record of publishing. Chairs who return to faculty status benefit from having maintained research momentum in the field.

What Are Common Obstacles?

Recalling the benefits of scholarly work may energize us, but a clear-eyed recognition of the obstacles a chair faces is necessary to help us strategize effectively. The struggles chairs experience in maintaining a research agenda differ more in intensity than in kind from those their faculty colleagues encounter. The challenges I'll describe here are familiar (at least in broad outline) to anyone who has ever tried to write a scholarly article. The most common challenges are rooted in issues of time, energy, and mindset.

Once you become chair, it is much more difficult to plan research time the way you might have done as a faculty member. On a daily basis, you'll typically perform a large number of brief tasks on a variety of issues, moving quickly from one focus to another, with few opportunities to block out large chunks of time.* Faculty administrators have far less control than their colleagues over the shape of their daily work; a constant stream

---

*Walter H. Gmelch and Val D. Miskin, *Chairing an Academic Department* (Thousand Oaks, CA: Sage, 1995), 131.

of small but urgent matters comes via email and phone, threatening to eat up every available moment.

New administrators may be particularly overwhelmed because of the learning curve that comes with the job. Chairs are also likely to receive service requests from outside their department, both on campus and from other institutions; typically, those in leadership roles tend to be asked to do more. An editor I used to work with likes to say, "When you need to get something done, ask a busy person." During the years I was chairing my department and serving on the Association of Departments of English Executive Committee, for instance, it was not uncommon for me to receive four, five, or six (or more) requests over the spring and summer for tenure or promotion reviews. (One year I foolishly agreed to six: it almost killed me.) Administrative tasks demand both time and energy, and an exhausted brain is not likely to be productive. Exhaustion often coincides with a disruption of work-life balance as well. As you mentor and respond to others' needs, you may not be receiving the mentorship and support you need to nurture your own intellectual development.

Finally, chairs may sometimes end up exacerbating the very obstacles that make their research more difficult. If the desire to bring tasks to completion is a priority, you may shy away from longer-horizon projects. Chairing can even be invoked as an excuse for a lack of research productivity: "I'd hoped to have that book finished by now, but I've been chairing my department." However, once you understand that the challenges are real, not a result of excuse-making or your imagination, you can move forward more productively and reflectively.

What Strategies or Tactics Can Help?

While no magic recipe exists to expand time, eliminate stressors, or strike an amazing balance in our lives, there is hope. By using smart strategies that address the obstacles chairs face, insisting that colleagues value your work as a scholar by sharing some of the administrative work with you, petitioning for resources that can provide support, and developing healthier habits and attitudes, you can indeed maintain a research profile.

Some of the most important strategies involve protecting blocks of time for scholarly work. The relative calm of the summer is helpful but is generally not enough. If you are given course release, the time that would have been devoted to teaching can be explicitly reallocated for scholarly work: one course released means that you might block out 5-10 hours each week in your schedule for your research. That might mean that you come in early and keep your door closed from 8:00 to 10:00 a.m. every day. It might mean creating an inviolable space in the week when you're in the lab with your students. It might mean that you stay off campus (and reply only to the most urgent of emails) one day a week. Different chairs have different needs and different work styles: organize some time when you are unavailable that works for you.

That said, while it's important to protect some of your time for research activities, that only works if you're otherwise available to your colleagues for departmental business. This raises the question of how much time a chair should spend in their department office each week. Should you set formal office hours—and if so, how many—or should you just generally "be around"? All institutions have guidelines or norms about office hours for students, but when it comes to chairs making themselves available to faculty colleagues, they are largely on their own. Twice when I came to departments from the outside to chair, it felt important to me to be very available. I was coming into troubled situations, and I knew it was important that faculty colleagues had full access—for the first year, that is. After that, I migrated to a schedule that allowed me a bit more discretionary time in my schedule. My preference has always been to be on campus for a pretty traditional, 9-5 work week and to block out times for classes, student office hours, other meetings, lunch, and time for reading and research. Any of the times not allocated to one of these tasks was then available for faculty to drop by with a question or concern or just for conversation. This year I am chairing a department across campus from my home department, so I'm not in the building very often, and it's taking a toll. I feel less like I know what's going on and how people are feeling; much of the daily texture of the department's operation is eluding me. It is unavoidable in this case, but it has resensitized me to the fact that there's just no substitute for being around. To a certain extent, quality time is quantity time.

You may also need to say no to requests even more often than you did as a full-time faculty member, and as Anne Lucas advises, you should make a habit of frequently delegating any "task that someone else can do."* Because administrative work easily expands to fill available time, you should schedule creative time before you schedule administrative time without feeling any guilt. After all, administrative work involves deadlines that ensure its completion, so you need to respond by putting in place structures that create urgency around your research and creative work too. Your commitment to research can be communicated in ways that "enlist the dean, the department secretary, and faculty members in the cause" and define research time as an appropriate departmental expectation.†

Managing email more effectively can help streamline administrative work. Sometimes answering an email message in person—walking down the hall rather than reflexively hitting reply—can resolve an issue at one go, preventing you from having to participate in a long email chain. Some chairs create email

---

*Ann F. Lucas, *Strengthening Departmental Leadership: A Team-Building Guide for Chairs in Colleges and Universities* (San Francisco: Jossey-Bass, 1994), 255.

†Lucas, *Strengthening Departmental Leadership*, 254. Since Lucas published her book, the term "secretary" has fallen from favor. Most academic departments now use the title department coordinator, academic coordinator, or program coordinator—or assistant—for the staff member who exercises an oversight role in the day-to-day operations of the department.

blackout periods, only answering at the start and end of the workday, for instance, or use programs that block or track time spent online. For some, simply turning off the feature of your program that dings every time a new message arrives is enough to keep email in its place. Too often, chairs are controlled by email instead of using it to work efficiently. Learning to prioritize and manage the inbox can help you avoid information overflow, and clear guidance is readily available in publications such as Mark Hurst's *Bit Literacy*.*

Knowing the changes to their workflow that will come with the new role, some chairs make the decision to change the nature of their research because of the difficulty of finding uninterrupted blocks of time. This change may involve setting "small, achievable goals" and finding ways to be productive in "sporadic chunks of 15 to 30 minutes,"† or it may involve taking on smaller or incremental projects. Instead of focusing on a book project, for instance, you might emphasize book reviews, journalistic pieces, or concise essays (although a series of conference papers could build gradually to a longer project). Instead of opening a new line of inquiry in your lab, you may need to be satisfied with keeping current research moving forward with the help of students. Some chairs turn their focus to what Ernest Boyer calls "the scholarship of administration"‡—the book you hold in your hands would be an example. Some may feel their enthusiasm for research renewed through collaboration with colleagues who are both distant and nearby. Whether they are writing together or meeting as a research group, participants are more likely to stay motivated when they are accountable to one another.

---

*Mark Hurst, *Bit Literacy: Productivity in the Age of E-mail* (New York: Creative Good, 2007).

†Hollis Phelps, "Doing Research at a Teaching-Focused College," *Inside Higher Ed*, September 13, 2013, https://www.insidehighered.com/advice/2013/09/13/how-do-good-research-teaching-intensive-institution-essay.

‡Ernest L. Boyer, *Scholarship Reconsidered: Priorities of the Professoriate* (Princeton, NJ: Carnegie Foundation for the Advancement of Teaching, 1990).

When you need to feel reenergized to get scholarly work done, a number of strategies can help. One is finding a protected space. Some chairs simply close their office door to focus on research, while others work from home or in a setting that is not associated with administrative or personal responsibilities. You can also find encouragement through professional and personal support systems. Colleagues, family, and friends can support a healthy work-life balance and provide breaks from administrative duties.

Even when you have found effective ways to manage your time and energy, you might find yourself stalled. The advice commonly offered about writing and procrastination, such as writing regularly and at a time of the day when our energy level is high—which is often the start of each day—may help here.[*] You need to analyze your own situation in order to determine what is holding you back from your research and what might help you move forward.

What Resources Can Chairs Seek?

While you can manage some of these strategies on our own, others will work best (or only) if external support is in place to help you manage your time, energy, and well-being. Release time, sabbaticals, administrative leave, days working from home, summers away, and other blocks of non-administrative time can help tremendously. Writing retreats seem to be especially effective for motivating participants,[†] and money can be set aside for this activity and for other kinds of professional development, research, and travel. Research assistants and grants can also be

[*]Robert Hauptman, "How to Be a Successful Scholar: Publish Efficiently," *Journal of Scholarly Publishing* 36, no. 2 (2005): 116.

[†]Sarah Moore, "Writers' Retreats for Academics: Exploring and Increasing the Motivation to Write," *Journal of Further and Higher Education* 27, no. 3 (2003): 333–342.

helpful supports. I've written in other chapters about the chair's role in advocating for these resources for faculty colleagues; don't neglect to make the case for your own research as well. Because you'd like to avoid the appearance of having secured research support for yourself at the expense of your colleagues, ideally these requests should be made of your dean at the time of your appointment and they should not be paid for with department funds.

Finally, some chairs choose to invest some of their own resources in direct and indirect research support, using part of the extra salary they may earn from their administrative work. This extra income can be used to secure a gym membership, housekeeping services, or a writing week in a cabin somewhere. Some research expenses may be deductible business expenses for those who itemize deductions on their taxes. Being physically, emotionally, and mentally healthy will enable you to handle the combination of administrative responsibilities, teaching, and research better.

Researching as Chair: Difficult but Not Impossible

Research expectations can vary greatly according to the particular faculty member and their context. Meeting with your dean to establish research goals can help you develop appropriate expectations. But you must also articulate your research agendas on the basis of personal and professional aspirations. You must not let a dean discourage you from pursuing your professional aspirations so that you'll have more time available for administrative tasks. That's a recipe for ending a term as chair with the feeling that your scholarly gifts have been squandered, sacrificed to administrative exigencies.

No matter what decisions you make regarding your research goals, you will have more peace about your work if you learn to value your administrative as well as your scholarly and teaching accomplishments. Too often, a voice in our head tells us that administration is "the dark side." That voice is cartoonish and needs to be shut down. Instead, find role models who continue to develop both their administrative and scholarly gifts and acknowledge that those gifts are not always mutually exclusive. Although he wouldn't be a role model for everyone, even all English professors, I paid careful attention during the six-year period when Stanley Fish, the colorful and controversial literary critic, chaired the English department at Duke University. He enjoyed administrative support that few of us can imagine while in the role, but he managed to publish one (600-page) book and fourteen articles or book chapters during that period. It's also helpful for us to make note of the changes we have effected through our administrative work that were the result of collaborative and institutional development rather than individual accomplishments.

Finally, institutions should more adequately recognize administrative work in promotion decisions so that chairs will be supported.* And when other people, including students, tell you you're doing a great job, believe them.

---

*Alexandra W. Logue, "The Scholarship of Administration," *Inside Higher Ed*, February 2, 2009, https://www.insidehighered.com/views/2009/02/02/scholar ship-administration; Council of Writing Program Administrators, "Evaluating the Intellectual Work of Writing Program Administration," July 17, 2019, https:// wpacouncil.org/aws/CWPA/pt/sd/news_article/242849/_PARENT/layout _details/false; MLA Commission on Professional Service, "Making Faculty Work Visible: Reinterpreting Professional Service, Teaching, and Research in the Fields of Language and Literature," *Profession* (1996): 161-216.

Chapter 11

Reinventing Yourself for Life after Chairing

Although a chair's appointment normally comes with a set contract term (three or five years is common), if you're doing a good job, your colleagues will be delighted to have you take on a second term or even a third. Beyond a certain point, though, your effectiveness is diminished. You're no longer bringing new ideas and new energy to the role and you're not allowing young leadership talent in your department an opportunity to develop. There is wisdom, that is to say, in knowing when it's time to step down. When you do, it's time to think about what you'd like the next chapter of your career to look like. For many, that's as simple as returning to full-time teaching and research while studiously avoiding any backseat-driver's advice to your successor. For others, the route may be up and out of the department to an interdisciplinary or interdepartmental program (as director), to the dean's office (as associate dean or dean), or even to another institution, as a chair, director, dean, or provost. In this chapter, I'll consider in turn the various rich options open to you.

Life after chairing looks very different depending on whether you found the chair's role rewarding. Some years ago I stepped down at the end of my contracted term as chair in order to take a sabbatical leave I had accrued and move a research project forward. Much to my surprise, as I have written about elsewhere,* midway through that leave year a chance conversation led me to realize that my chairing days weren't done yet, and I returned from sabbatical for another term (much to the relief of the chair who had stepped in for me, who absolutely hated the job). If my term as chair had been dispiriting, depleting, or felt like one long distraction from my true calling, planning for the future would have looked very different. (I'd served a term like that as chair elsewhere, and by the end I was literally counting the days until my release.) There's no point in mincing words about this: chairing is not for everyone, even if many are called upon to serve.

If you've served a term as chair and have not found the work rewarding, then probably you've met your obligation and can call it quits. Many institutions provide sabbatical or administrative leave as a cushion for those leaving the chair's role, a time to regroup and refocus their energies. If this is not something customarily offered to chairs at your institution, consider asking for a sabbatical leave at the successful conclusion of your term as chair when you're negotiating the terms of your appointment.† That period away from the department serves at least two good

---

*Kevin J. H. Dettmar, "Don't Cry for Me, Academia!" *Chronicle of Higher Education*, June 27, 2016, https://www.chronicle.com/article/dont-cry-for-me-academia/.

†Funny story: when I came to the school where I now teach as an outside chair hire, I made such a demand as a term of my acceptance of the job. The dean wanted me to agree to two consecutive three-year terms in order to provide stability for the department; in return, I asked for a sabbatical leave at the conclusion of my term as chair. After pretending (?) to give my request some hard thought, the dean agreed to my terms. Only some months later did I learn that the period of leave I had asked for—which would have seemed quite generous at the institution I was leaving—was in fact the standard leave policy for the faculty I was joining. There are probably a couple of lessons here, including "Study the faculty handbook."

purposes. First, and most important, you've just concluded a demanding period of service. If you've served well, you've put the needs of your faculty colleagues and your department's students ahead of your own and you're probably a bit the worse for wear. A term (or more) out of the office and out of the classroom provides the space you need to recover. It also provides an uncluttered time when you can set new goals, whether that means developing a new course, reviving a stalled project, or launching a new project. Finally—and this is also important—it gives the new chair a bit of space for discovering their own style and priorities without the pressure of the former chair looking over their shoulder. Of course it's also important to be available to the new chair (within the limits of your comfort) for the questions they'll inevitably have in their early weeks and months. A reliable (and long-serving) department staff administrator is a great help as the institutional memory and a department handbook (including bylaws) is important for ensuring that policies are fair and uniform, but no one has the practical and recent experience of chairing the department that you do.

Even if your institution is forward thinking and generous enough to grant—or you were cunning enough to negotiate—a term of leave after your term as chair, you will eventually need to be reintegrated into your department's culture as a regular faculty member, unless you move immediately into another administrative role (see below). For many of us, though, even a period of sitting out doesn't quite quell our desire to weigh in on important departmental matters—and of course, as a full member of the faculty, you have as much right to your opinion and your vote as any of your colleagues. As much, but not more: the title for a former department chair is simply "professor." Especially if your successor makes any decisions or takes any positions that are unpopular with any portion of the department—that is to say, if they are a human being—you will find colleagues trying to draft you to their side of the dispute as some kind of authority or expert witness on How Things Ought to Be Done. (It never fails: even colleagues who were disgruntled while you were chair will try to recruit you to their side of arguments once you've stepped down.) Resist. If you see your successor taking an ill-considered path and you can be certain that your motives are pure, talk with them privately and give them your two cents' worth—and then shut up. Practice calling them your "successor"; it will remind you that you want them to succeed. Don't fall prey to the kind of egotism that secretly wishes for their failure as indirect proof of your own success. It's not.

If you're a person for whom a term as chair was what my late colleague David Foster Wallace might call "a supposedly fun thing I'll never do again," then that's it. Shake it off, get back into your teaching and research, and don't make yourself a nuisance to your successor.

Seeking Further Leadership Roles

But for some of us, it's not that easy. I remember quite vividly a former department chair I knew early in my career. He had served a very successful term as chair of his department and enjoyed a fair bit of power and influence on campus; chairing suited him. But his time as chair came to a sudden end when behavior in his private life off campus came to light and ran smack into a small town, a university, and a dean with zero tolerance for such things. He was unceremoniously sent back into the faculty with no further opportunities for leadership at the institution. Bill's professional identity was as chair of his department and he had been stripped of it. Instead of simply accepting the inevitable and returning quietly to the faculty, though, Bill remained frustrated at being locked out of decision-making roles. As I write these words, Mike Trout of the Los Angeles Angels, the greatest baseball player of his era, is on the injured list with a calf strain. Seeing him watching the games from the dugout, unable to participate physically in the game (and as bad as the Angels are with Mike Trout, they're just terrible without him), is kind of heartbreaking. And Bill had been consigned, permanently, to the "injured list."

What are the options for those who are eager to get back into academic leadership after serving a stint as chair? For some, a rewarding next step involves finding another way to represent their department's needs and priorities to the larger campus community, either through leadership in faculty shared-governance structures or by seeking an administrative position at the school, college, or university level. Roles that support the faculty voice in shared governance are typically uncompensated, except perhaps at very large institutions; this is volunteer service, similar to service on various faculty committees. Structures differ across institutional types, but many shared-governance models feature a faculty senate. Service on the senate, either as a member at large elected by the faculty or in a leadership role (probably after some time there), is a great way both to learn more about administrative processes on your campus and to bring back information to your colleagues in the department about new initiatives the administration is proposing. Campuses with a unionized faculty will have a parallel set of structures to support the faculty association that will provide additional opportunities to serve your colleagues during negotiations with the administration. Institutions that enroll graduate students will also typically have some sort of graduate council, a kind of parallel structure to the faculty senate that focuses exclusively on issues pertaining to graduate education.

The other leadership track available to faculty with chair experience is college or university administration—the office of the dean, the office of the provost, or the office of the dean of graduate studies (this constellation will look different at different institutions). Associate (or assistant) dean positions within these units are typically filled internally and are a logical stepping-stone for those ultimately interested in the positions to which they report—dean (of the faculty or of the college), graduate dean, and provost. Those senior leadership positions—vice-presidential positions in many institutional structures—are sometimes filled from the faculty and sometimes selected through a national search, often with the help of a search firm. Time served as an associate dean will stand you in good stead if you decide that you're interested in the dean's position and it's filled through an internal search. Once a national search is decided on, though, all bets are off: too often the local candidates are (consciously or unconsciously) discounted in favor of the shiny new outsider. I suspect that the odds worsen further with a search firm: they're being paid handsomely for their consultation (often 33% of the position's annual salary), and if they help "find" a candidate already sitting comfortably in the building next door, it's not clear that they've quite earned their fee.

Moving On

The final possibility is to go external yourself. In a tight job market for professors, many faculty find it difficult to move at mid-career due to the scarcity of job openings for tenured professors. The one occasional exception to this pattern is positions for someone to come in from outside the institution to chair a department (an outside chair). These opportunities can enable you to move to an institution that's more desirable, whether professionally or personally (or both), and they can sometimes provide a salary bump that would not be possible at your current institution. Often such positions are relatively open in terms of disciplinary subspecialty; the department is hiring someone with experience and skills in chairing a department, not macroeconomics or computational linguistics. I've twice been able to move to institutions and parts of the country that were better suited to my work and my family's needs because I was willing to chair the department I hoped to join. (Indeed, in one red-letter year, I was offered three different chairs jobs and was able to take my pick.) These are not opportunities that my standing as a scholar in my field would have afforded me; rather, departments convinced their deans that they needed someone to come in and do some heavy lifting and I was willing—and qualified—to do it.

That scenario also contains a coded warning, however. There may be exceptions (although I'm not aware of any), but happy, healthy, high-functioning departments don't require a new tenure line from the administration in order to get someone to chair them. Departments that conduct a national search for chair are departments in crisis. Sometimes the crisis is quite literally that—a crisis, not a chronic problem—and some committed work up front can create the conditions in the department that you'll be happy to work under when your term is up. Sometimes, for instance, a demographic shift in the department—a bimodal distribution of very senior faculty, some on the verge of retirement and a cohort of untenured junior faculty—creates a temporary leadership vacuum that an outside chair can fill. But often divisions within the department have made it impossible for either side to put forward a candidate for chair who is acceptable to the majority of the department faculty.

Needless to say, these are dangerous situations to walk into. Unless you're quite lucky, it will be difficult for you as a candidate to get a reliable read on what's amiss in the department and whether you'd be able—or willing—to help. Dysfunctional departments are unlikely to go public with any of their interpersonal grievances. Your on-campus interview with the dean or provost may provide you with a bit more candor. You might, if it doesn't seem too aggressive under the circumstances, ask for a copy of the most recent department self-study and outside review, which may call attention to some long-standing problems. But ultimately, if you're offered the position, you're going to have to make a judgment call. You know what the upside might be (in terms of location, salary, quality of students, and institutional culture, strengths, and resources, for example), and you'll have to weigh that against an ill-defined downside. One minor hedge that faculty faced with such a decision often make is to ask their current institution to give them a yearlong leave without pay, although not all institutions will countenance this (and sometimes the receiving institution will not accept you under such circumstances). Ideally, though, the leave gives you a first year (or most of it) at your new institution to assess whether or not it's going to work out—and if it's not, there's still the possibility (albeit not a hugely attractive one) to skulk back to your former institution with your tail between your legs.

Finally, a further word about search firms. I'm not aware of them ever being used for department chair searches, but if you have your eyes set on a bigger prize—dean or provost at another institution—odds are you'll have to start working with them. Indeed, during your time as chair you may well start getting emails from search firms to let you know that your name has been put forward for an opportunity, ask whether you'd be interested in applying, and if you are, suggest an initial phone conversation. If you think you might be interested in moving for an administrative job at some point in the near to medium term, take the call, even if you're not sure you're interested in the position in question. Search firms make their money by providing candidates for administrative positions—some suggested by members of the institution's search committee, yes, but some drawn from the firm's database. If you're interested in leadership opportunities and would be willing (or eager) to leave your current position, you want to be suggested for positions as they come open. These search firms also keep listings of open searches they're assisting in on their web sites, and in theory, you can learn about administrative openings this way. However, typically applications that come to a department "cold" (that is, on your own initiative) instead of through a suggestion by the search committee or the search consultants have little chance of being seriously considered.

The Road Less Traveled

At the point that you're first asked to consider chairing your department—by your colleagues or by your dean—you face a fork in the road. Will you deemphasize your teaching and research or creative work, at least for a time, to provide leadership to your colleagues? In some ways, the argument of this chapter is that if you've chosen the leadership path and completed a term (or multiple terms) as chair, you're confronted with another fork: more leadership or less? More investment in your students and your scholarship or more investment in your colleagues and your institution (or new colleagues at a new institution)? They're both very good choices, of course, and your time as chair should have given you a pretty good idea about which path you now want to follow. If you'd like to take a short-term deep dive into higher education administration, there are two very valuable programs that may be available to you with your institution's help, one much shorter than the other. The quick one is the two-week Management Development Program offered by the Harvard Institutes for Higher Education.* The MDP covers all aspects of the dean's and provost's roles and responsibilities. It requires a nomination from your institution's president and it's not cheap, so your institution would also need to commit to covering the cost of the program for you. On a larger scale, the fellowships from the American Council on Education allow faculty members a year's leave from their home institution to embed with a senior administrator at another institution and work on projects. These fellowships (really a kind of professional internship) are frequently stepping-stones to administrative jobs in higher education. Here too you'll need to be nominated by your institution, which will also have to cover your salary for the year of your fellowship. (This is often managed in the form of a sabbatical leave.)

For some of us, chairing is something we do—whether willingly or grudgingly or well or poorly. For others, chair is who we are

---

*"Management Development Program (MDP)," Harvard Graduate School of Education, https://www.gse.harvard.edu/ppe/program/management-develop ment-program-mdp.

in a very real sense. And there's no very good way to be sure which describes you until you've done a stretch in the saddle. If you're a one-and-done chair, congratulations and enjoy your migration back into the professoriate. If instead you've found that the challenges and responsibilities and affordances of chairing your department speak to something deep within you, good news: the academy needs more people like you. Your challenge now is to find the right opportunity to serve further.

Department Chairing and the Gift of Service

Some years ago I was tapped as a last-minute replacement for the distinguished literary and cultural critic Michael Bérubé as part of the "State of the Profession" colloquium hosted by the University of Colorado, Boulder. When the invitation came, I reached out to Michael and he replied, with a characteristic wisecrack, "I was just going to argue that professors should be more like Snape. I'm sure you can do much better than that." I'm not sure about "better," but I did make a very different argument, so I adopted a different Harry Potter character as my avatar. My argument that day was that professors need to be more like Prof. Pomona Sprout, a rather less prominent character in the Harry Potter series than Snape—a candidate, perhaps, for Best Supporting Actress rather than Best Actor. Prof. Sprout works primarily behind the scenes in the Harry Potter novels. We learn only in the epilogue to the final volume that her pupil, Neville Longbottom, has become professor of herbology at Hogwarts owing to Sprout's quiet support.

To close this book, I want to focus again on this supporting role. In one of its guises it's what, in common parlance, we refer to as the department chair.

I'd like to talk about the underground economy of the scholarly gift, an economy that runs silently, invisibly alongside—or better, underneath—the academy's official economy of prestige. This gift economy is the black market to the economy of prestige, what has come to be called the "star system" of academia—the world of what Jeffrey Williams has dubbed "academostars."* According to Stanley Fish, who ought to know, the star system is fueled by this prestige: "I think the star system," he explains in an interview with Williams, "is inevitable given that the coin or currency of the profession is in part prestige, so what you expect stars to do is to attract graduate student and to make a program more visible."† It will not do, however, to oppose in any simplistic way the economy of the gift to the academy's reigning economy of prestige, for this gift economy is not entirely divorced from the economy of prestige. Without at least some prestige, a scholar has no meaningful gift to give, no entrée into the world in which they might wish to do some good. To be capable of real scholarly gifts, we'll have to put our CVs in order, too.

Inevitably, superstars have become the visible public face of the profession. The American public doesn't often understand, and even less frequently tries to understand, the work we do, and to be honest, we have not been very good about explaining it to them. But the fair hair and broad smile of Pomona alum and Nobel laureate Jennifer Doudna, the deceptively reassuring grin of Noam Chomsky, and the boyish good looks of Michael Bérubé are instantly legible. I'm well aware of the controversies

*This was the title of the special issue of the *Minnesota Review* Williams edited in 2001.

†Jeffrey J. Williams, "Stanley Agonistes: An Interview with Stanley Fish," *Minnesota Review*, n.s., 52–54 (Fall 2001): 115.

surrounding the notion of an academic star system. Too often the term "star system" reflects a kind of anti-intellectual conservatism and is used to suggest that all of us, or nearly all of us, are divas, unworthy of the lavish salaries and research support we receive in the ongoing bidding war for our services we call our professional lives. Williams calls the notion of an academic star system "our present professional imaginary,"* and in this he's surely right. But whatever we choose to call it, we'd all have to admit, I think, that there's a rather wide (and possibly widening) gap between the best and worst compensated teachers in the academy. The ratio isn't as obscene as that between the CEOs of major American corporations and their employees, but even on some public university campuses, the salaries of the stars can be double and even triple those of their less high-profile colleagues with comparable seniority. To point this out is not to begrudge Lawrence Summers his salary, but surely we cannot pretend that there are no stars in the academic firmament. Many are called, but few are chosen.

But I'm concerned about our common life together, what Virginia Woolf calls "the common life which is the real life and not of the little separate lives which we live as individuals."† In her foreword to Marcel Mauss's *The Gift*, Mary Douglas writes: "According to Mauss . . . a gift that does nothing to enhance solidarity is a contradiction."‡ But nothing about the ethical imperative to perform the kind of service I'll be talking about here was ever conveyed to me as a graduate student. We can do better for our graduate students. This is perhaps one practical application of the philosophizing to follow.

*Williams, "Stanley Agonistes, 118.
†Virginia Woolf, *A Room of One's Own* (1929; repr., New York: Harcourt Brace, 1957), 117.
‡Marcel Mauss, *The Gift: The Form and Reason for Exchange in Archaic Societies*, translated by W. D. Halls (1950; repr., New York: W. W. Norton: 1990), vii.

What I'd like to advocate here is what I'm calling an economy of the scholarly gift—not in the sense that the *Encyclopedia Britannica* is scholarly but in the narrow sense of a gift that scholars exchange among one another. All modern thinking about the gift is related, more or less directly, to the groundbreaking ethnography Mauss published in 1923-1924. Mauss's signal claim is that there is no such thing as a free gift:

> It is indeed ownership that one obtains with the gift that one receives. But it is ownership of a certain kind. One could say that it partakes of all kinds of legal principles that we, more modern, have carefully isolated from one another. It is ownership and possession, a pledge and something hired out, a thing sold and bought, and at the same time deposited, mandated, and bequeathed in order to be passed on to another. For it is only given you on condition that you make use of it for another or pass it on to a third person, the "distant partner."*

I want for the moment to place a bookmark at the phrase "a third person"—the gift is "only given you on the condition that you make use of it for another or pass it on to a third person."

Following Mauss's insight that "a gift is received 'with a burden attached,'"† I want to sketch out this economy of the scholarly gift. An "ordinary" gift puts me under obligation to repay the giver; the title of the first subsection of Mauss's introduction is "The Gift, and Especially the Obligation to Return It."‡ But scholarly gifts are different. These are the gifts we receive from those "above" us in the profession, whether they are of higher rank, have more seniority or greater professional stature, or are associated with a more prestigious institution. That, in part, is what makes the gift of a letter of recommendation, for instance, so valuable. But here's

*Mauss, *The Gift*, 23-24.
†Mauss, *The Gift*, 41.
‡Mauss, *The Gift*, 1.

the paradox: although I'm deeply grateful for these gifts, there's no way I can repay them directly because my "coin" is no good in their realm. The scholarly gift is characterized by a dynamic of asymmetrical reciprocity: an ethical obligation to give back is combined with a structural inability to repay directly those I owe.

How, then, do we even begin to pay back these scholarly gifts? The answer, in short, is that we turn around and pay them down the line: pay them to younger or less well-positioned scholars we are in a position to help. Which is to say that the profession runs, albeit secretly, on an intergenerational economy of debt and indebtedness, an exchange of quiet acts of professional courtesy and generosity. And this deep well of debt and indebtedness is, in the final analysis, a good rather than a bad thing.

It's important, for my purposes, to distinguish between the gift of the mentor from the gift of the peer or colleague. We talk about and understand collegiality, even if we're often not very good at practicing it. Collegiality, however, is an example of symmetrical reciprocity, whereas the scholarly gift is characterized by asymmetrical reciprocity. And this exchange of gifts between unequals remains undiscussed. I'm talking not primarily about generosity toward students, important—crucial—though that is, but about generosity toward peers and colleagues (although at the upper end of the spectrum, of course, the boundary between graduate student and colleague is both fuzzy and fluid). Perhaps it's more useful to differentiate the kind of generosity that is more or less obligatory, implicitly a condition of employment (serving on dissertation committees, writing letters of recommendation when asked) from what we might call entrepreneurial generosity, a professional generosity that actively searches for colleagues to invest in. It's a question, perhaps, of devoting our scholarly capital to those who have less, with the understanding that they'll at some point turn around and make that same investment in others.

I'm willing to bet that anyone reading this book has been the recipient of untold, and sometimes unmerited, professional gifts. The consciousness of this debt implants a desire to pay it back, but you can't pay it back. You can only—and I apologize in advance for the motivational-poster phrase—pay it forward.

The phrase is freighted with untoward associations owing, in particular, to a cloying, maudlin movie of that title, but the concept is much older, as is the term. In the world of finance, an arrangement in which a debtor makes a new loan instead of repaying the lender is called "paying it forward." Robert Heinlein is sometimes credited with coining the phrase in his 1951 novel *Between Planets*. Benjamin Franklin, without the nomenclature, clearly advocated for the practice in this 1784 letter to Benjamin Webb:

> I send you herewith a Bill for Ten Louis d'ors. I do not pretend to *give* such a Sum. I only *lend* it to you. . . . When you meet with another honest Man in similar Distress, you must pay me by lending this Sum to him; enjoyning him to discharge the Debt by a like operation when he shall be able and shall meet with another opportunity.—I hope it may thus go thro' many hands before it meets with a Knave that will stop its Progress. This is a Trick of mine for doing a deal of good with a little money.*

When it comes to the gifts we've received from our mentors in the profession, we must pay them forward because there's no way for us to pay them back.

We can do this in many ways: writing letters of recommendation; agreeing to do outside tenure reviews; reading the manuscripts of colleagues, both for colleagues we know and for journals and presses; providing book reviews; serving in scholarly organizations; or contributing to collective publishing projects that don't immediately or obviously burnish our scholarly reputations. And most especially, given the focus of this book, agreeing—even

---

*Benjamin Franklin to Benjamin Webb, April 22, 1784, Founders Online, https://founders.archives.gov/documents/Franklin/01-42-02-0117; italics in original. Webb was mostly likely a London merchant; he had served as a director of the London Assurance Co. when Franklin wrote this letter. See Benjamin Webb to Benjamin Franklin, December 25, 1777, Founders Online, https://founders.archives.gov/documents/Franklin/01-25-02-0272.

stepping forward—to chair your department. One of the most famous invocations of the gift in the Western tradition is Paul's statement in the book of Romans: "The free gift of God is eternal life through Jesus Christ our Lord." The Greek word for "free gift" in that passage is "charisma." To the extent that we have any charisma, any star cachet, we need to turn it into a gift. Chair your department and share it with your colleagues.

This is the unpaid labor by which our profession remains professional. And just like most of our scholarly work, these works of generosity are done when we're off the clock—at night, on weekends, during unpaid summer months. What are the institutional, structural rewards for this service? Well they're just awful, of course—but perhaps that's not the point.

It is my sincerest wish here at the close that I would be able to give you a gift. It is possible to suggest that, contra the craven (if hilarious) academic world conjured up by the likes of David Lodge, Jane Smiley, and Richard Russo, the real energy that fuels our profession isn't jealousy or infighting, but something we might quaintly dub collegiality. W. B. Yeats, a control freak, took the liberty of writing his own epitaph; indeed, he practically wrote his entire funeral service in the poem "Under Ben Bulben," which ends with the lines that would be inscribed on his gravestone: "Cast a cold eye / On life, on death—/ Horseman, pass by!"*

But there's at least one other embedded epitaph, or perhaps it's better described as a eulogy, in Yeats's poetry, one that is more interesting for our purposes. It comes in the closing lines of his poem "The Municipal Gallery Revisited." The poem's narrative rehearses a visit to the Dublin art gallery where portraits of some of Yeats's eminent friends and colleagues hang, including his benefactor Lady Augusta Gregory and the playwright J. M. Synge. Having walked us through the gallery with him and testified to the greatness of those remembered there, Yeats closes this way:

*W. B. Yeats, *The Poems: A New Edition*, edited by Richard J. Finneran (New York: Macmillan, 1983), 328.

You that would judge me, do not judge alone
This book or that, come to this hallowed place
Where my friends' portraits hang and look thereon;
Ireland's history in their lineaments trace;
Think where man's glory most begins and ends,
And say my glory was I had such friends.*

Try replacing "friends" with "colleagues," and this epitaph might appear on the Tomb of the Unknown Department Chair.

For some of us, at a certain point in our careers, administrative work is no longer something to dread or to apologize for. For some of us, serving as chair of a department or dean of a college comes unbidden as a second, midcareer calling. Too often, perhaps, it calls us away from the work we were destined to do, and those tend to be the stories we hear. But sometimes, taking on administrative duties is precisely the culmination and fulfillment of that scholarly work, allowing us to recognize our past as prologue for the first time.

We don't talk enough about the fact that besides representing an obligation or a noble sacrifice, academic administration can be a calling; that the work can be incredibly rewarding instead of draining or distracting; that while it requires training and accomplishment as a scholar to qualify for such an appointment, success in it relies on a set of gifts that, for the most part, have nothing to do with those that sent us off to graduate school in the first place.

Administration is a category of academic work that faculty reward systems refuse to recognize adequately. We're taught from early on how to value our accomplishments as scholars, and we choose mentors whose research has distinguished them in their fields. At most prestigious colleges and universities, good teaching alone won't suffice to establish a distinguished career, but every institution worth its salt at least professes to care about

*Yeats, *The Poems*, 321.

teaching and very publicly rewards it. It's easy enough, then, to feel good about being a good teacher, and it's certainly in that guise that an often-hostile public likes us best.

But academic administration is abject: it requires gifts that one apologizes for possessing. I'm still vaguely embarrassed every time I send someone a spreadsheet as an email attachment. I probably feel that way more acutely than most owing to the particulars of my situation. I'm something of a stowaway. In the late summer of my career I got to move to an institution the likes of which I'd only daydreamed about. I didn't get my position here because my name was on everyone's lips and my books in everyone's offices. No, I snuck in through the servant's entrance as a department chair.

Being good at academic administration paradoxically makes one feel bad about oneself. Surely this is wrong. What I'm advocating here is not a prescription for every PhD. It's a path for only some of us. But for those few—having taught well, published articles and papers and books, and created a scholarly identity—the next challenge and source of career fulfillment lies in taking on the job of hiring and mentoring younger scholars and devoting our experience to the task of clearing obstacles for them so that they might enjoy the same rewards and fulfillment as scholars and teachers that we have.

There's a lot more to good chairing than just faculty mentoring, of course, even if that's the piece I most relish. It falls to chairs to provide leadership and vision for a department, to facilitate the discussion around questions such as: What kind of department do we want to be? How might our curriculum change to keep pace with our evolving field and changing student population? What is our department's role in the larger college or university community? How might we provide intellectual leadership for the campus? That's who I am now—a senior professor who has done scholarly work that I'm proud of (and will do more) and who deeply values his relationships with students but whose most rewarding challenge these days involves facilitating the work of my colleagues.

Index